COOL RESTAURANTS
THE COOKBOOK

teNeues

Imprint

Produced by fusion publishing GmbH, Stuttgart . Los Angeles   www.fusion-publishing.com

Editorial team: Haike Falkenberg (Biographies, Editor), Anna Koor (Biographies, Introduction, Editor)
Katharina Feuer (Editorial coordination, Layout)
Sabine Scholz (Text coordination)
Übersetzungsbüro RR Communications (Translations)
Undercover Visuelle Kommunikationsgesellschaft mbH, Jan Hausberg (Prepress + imaging)

Cover photo (location): Martin Nicholas Kunz (Spice Market, New York)

Back cover photos from top to bottom (location): Michael Kleinberg (Gilt), courtesy Gilt (foodshot), Martin Nicholas Kunz (Spice Market), Michael Link für CPA! Wiesbaden (foodshot Spice Market), courtesy Sketch (Sketch), Peter Clayman (foodshot Sketch)

Photos (location): Markus Bachmann, samba (Lary Fary, Zheng He's), Roland Bauer (Aux Gazelles, Käfer-Schänke), Peter Clayman (foodshot Sketch), courtesy bacar (bacar), courtesy The China House (The China House), courtesy Fasano p50, 55 (Fasano), courtesy Gilt (foodshot Gilt), courtesy Patagonia Sur p110, 115 (Patagonia Sur), courtesy Restaurant Imperial (Restaurant Imperial), courtesy CL3 Architects and Shangri-La Hotel, Beijing (Nishimura), courtesy Sketch (Sketch), Simon Dean (Fifteen), Gaia Group (Isola bar & grill), Gavin Jackson (Fasano, Patagonia Sur), Michael Kleinberg (Gilt), Kofler & Kompanie AG (K&K KOCHBAR), Martin Nicholas Kunz (Japonais, Spice Market), Oetomo Photography (Puro), Peter Paige (Amalia), Lukas Roth (FACIL Restaurant), Steve Theodorou, Vanessa Grobler, Simon Phipps, Matthew Donaldson (Canteen), Jörg Tietje (Centrale Restaurant Lounge)

All other foodshots by Michael Link für CPA! Wiesbaden
All other portraits courtesy of restaurant

Published by teNeues Publishing Group

teNeues Verlag GmbH + Co. KG
Am Selder 37
47906 Kempen, Germany
Tel.: 0049-(0)2152-916-0
Fax: 0049-(0)2152-916-111
E-mail: books@teneues.de

teNeues France S.A.R.L.
93, rue Bannier
45000 Orléans, France
Tel.: 0033-2-38541071
Fax: 0033-2-38625340

teNeues Publishing Company
16 West 22nd Street
New York, NY 10010, USA
Tel.: 001-212-627-9090
Fax: 001-212-627-9511

teNeues Publishing UK Ltd.
P.O. Box 402
West Byfleet
KT14 7ZF, Great Britain
Tel.: 0044-1932-403509
Fax: 0044-1932-403514

Press department: arehn@teneues.de
Tel.: 0049-(0)2152-916-202

www.teneues.com

ISBN: 978-3-8327-9271-8

© 2008 teNeues Verlag GmbH + Co. KG, Kempen

Printed in Italy

Bibliographic information published by Die Deutsche Bibliothek. Die Deutsche Bibliothek lists this publication in the Deutsche Nationalbibliografie; detailed bibliographic data is available in the Internet at http://dnb.ddb.de.

Content	Recipe	Page
Content	**Recipe**	**Page**
Introduction		5

Introduction

The art of cooking has, in recent years, risen beyond the confines of fad and fashion, nutrition and nourishment, to be granted cultural status of the highest order. Today, our food and eating habits tell us about who we are and define our aspirations perhaps more than any other facet of our lives.

Now—and no doubt for years to come—there is genuine global concern about the provenance of the food we consume: how local it has been sourced, how seasonal it is, and how long ago it was either still breathing or growing. Of course many of the world's top chefs have been operating this way for years, but since gastronomy has become part of the cultural mainstream the focus on authenticity has resonated with many of us, particularly the home cooking enthusiast. This has been helped by far wider accessibility to alternative ingredients and produce—whether it be unconventional cuts of meat, exotic seafood, wild plants, or unusual herbs, spices, and berries.

While there are galaxies of best-selling recipe books to sate the keen domestic cook, this collection will appeal to those who are fired by an ambition to thrill and inspire above and beyond the average dinner table. These celebrated chefs have shared some of their favorite dishes and many are signature creations that their restaurants are famous for. All the recipes have been tried and tested, so with a little preparation and skill, they can be assembled by the amateur cook at home.

However, our memories of the ultimate dining experience aren't limited to what arrives on the plate. It's a marriage of many factors that stir all the senses. It might start with a glamorous entrance, and then be a visual connection with a show kitchen, how a dish is presented on the plate, the sounds and sights of the surroundings and other diners, and the service one engages with. Recreating this drama in the privacy of home might be a challenge. However our lifestyles have not only influenced how we shop for food but transformed the architecture and interiors we live in. The kitchen has taken over the heart of the house and increasingly it's where we eat, live, play, study, and entertain, therefore providing every opportunity for budding gastronomes to indulge their skills in front of family and friends.

That said, the combination of nurtured technique and process, as well as culinary artistry, will always be the natural domain of the master chef. Yet this book peels away some of the hidden layers to reveal more about what composes the perfect dining experience. To the gastronomic elite of the restaurant world, food is theater—and that extends to the polished ambiance of the surroundings and sometimes the dynamic showmanship of the kitchen. These restaurants have been handpicked because they all make strong style statements—design has made a major contribution to their reputation and success.

What is apparent from this book is how diverse these professional chefs are, and how important it is for them to have the freedom to express their personalities through their food. Ask each of these chefs to create the perfect club sandwich or humita and the result will be 22 different interpretations, each imbued with that chef's heritage, upbringing, culture and training. Your creation will be different again. Most importantly, the recipes featured here have been reproduced in these renowned kitchens around the world countless times—refined and tweaked to perfection.

Thanks to the evolving vocabulary and culture of modern cuisine, today's top chefs lean towards a philosophy of simplicity, honesty and innovation in their cooking. So provided the amateur home cook is prepared to seek out the freshest quality ingredients and learn from these chefs about what works together in terms of flavors and textures, success will come naturally.

Anna Koor

Einleitung

Einst als kurzfristige Modeerscheinung abgetan, auf Nahrung und Lebensmittel beschränkt, hat sich die Kunst des Kochens in den letzten Jahren über diese Grenzen hinweggesetzt und mittlerweile höchsten Kulturstatus erreicht. Heute sagen uns unsere Ernährungs- und Essgewohnheiten, wer wir sind, und vielleicht mehr als jeder andere Bereich unseres Lebens definieren sie unser Streben und unsere Sehnsüchte.

In der heutigen Zeit, zweifelsohne auch in den kommenden Jahren, ist es uns allen ein ehrliches Anliegen zu erfahren, woher das Essen auf unserem Teller stammt: Wie lokal und saisonal ist das Erzeugnis wirklich? Wann atmete bzw. wuchs es noch? Für viele der besten Spitzenköche weltweit ist ein solches Verhalten natürlich nicht neu. Seit die Gastronomie aber Teil einer allgemeinen, kulturellen Bewegung geworden ist, ist Authentizität auch für viele von uns, vor allem für die Hobbyköche, in den Mittelpunkt gerückt. Begünstigt wurde diese Entwicklung durch erweiterte Möglichkeiten, an alternative Zutaten und Produkten zu kommen – ob es sich nun um ungewöhnliche Stücke vom Fleisch, exotischen Fisch und Meeresfrüchte, wilde Pflanzen oder ausgefallene Kräuter, Gewürze und Beeren handelt.

Es gibt ein riesiges Angebot an Kochbüchern, die sich bestens verkaufen und den Hunger des eifrigen Freizeitkochs stillen. An der vorliegenden Sammlung werden aber vor allem diejenigen ihre Freude haben, deren Ambition es ist, mit einem außergewöhnlichen Mahl für Begeisterung und Inspiration zu sorgen. Die in diesem Buch vorgestellten namhaften Küchenchefs haben uns einige ihrer Lieblingsgerichte verraten; viele davon sind typische kulinarische Schöpfungen, für die ihr Restaurant bekannt ist. Alle Rezepte wurden ausprobiert und getestet, sodass der Amateurkoch diese zu Hause mit ein wenig Vorbereitung und Können nachkochen kann.

Das ultimative Genusserlebnis im Restaurant beschränkt sich allerdings nicht auf das, was auf unserem Teller liegt. Vielmehr ist es ein Zusammenspiel verschiedener Aspekte, das alle unsere Sinne anspricht. Das kann beispielsweise ein glanzvoller Eingangsbereich sein, eine einsehbare Schauküche, die Präsentation des Gerichts auf dem Teller, die Geräusche und das Erscheinungsbild der Umgebung, die anderen Gäste und der Service. Diese Atmosphäre in den eigenen vier Wänden nachzubilden, kann durchaus eine Herausforderung darstellen. Mit unserem Lebensstil hat sich jedoch nicht nur die Art und Weise, wie wir Nahrungsmittel einkaufen verändert, sondern auch die Architektur und Innenausstattung des Umfelds, in dem wir leben. Die Küche ist zum Mittelpunkt des Hauses geworden; hier essen, leben, spielen, arbeiten wir und empfangen Gäste. So bietet dieser Raum dem Gastronom in spe auch die Möglichkeit, sein Können vor Familie und Freunden unter Beweis zu stellen.

Nichtsdestoweniger werden bestimmte erlernte Techniken und Arbeitsabläufe ebenso wie kulinarische Kunstfertigkeit immer das natürliche Terrain des professionellen Meisterkochs bleiben. Dennoch, dieser Band legt einige versteckte Aspekte frei und wir erfahren mehr über das, was das perfekte kulinarische Erlebnis ausmacht. Für die gastronomische Elite der Restaurantwelt ist Essen ein großes Schauspiel – und das erstreckt sich bis zum ausgefeilten Ambiente der Umgebung und manchmal auch bis zur dynamischen Zurschaustellung der Küche. Die hier aufgeführten Restaurants wurden ausgewählt, weil sie alle klare Stilaussagen machen – das Design hat ganz wesentlich zu ihrem Ansehen und Erfolg beigetragen.

An diesem Buch lässt sich sehr schön ablesen, wie unterschiedlich die professionellen Köche sind und wie wichtig es ihnen ist, die Freiheit zu haben, durch ihre Gerichte ihre Persönlichkeit auszudrücken. Würde man jeden dieser Köche bitten, das perfekte Club-Sandwich oder eine Humita zuzubereiten, das Ergebnis wären 22 verschiedene Interpretationen – jede von ihnen geprägt von Herkunft, Kultur und Ausbildung des Kochs. Und auch Ihre eigene Kreation wird wiederum ganz anders ausfallen. Betonen möchten wir, dass die hier vorgestellten Rezepte in den renommierten Küchen weltweit unzählige Male gekocht wurden – verbessert und verfeinert bis zur Perfektion.

Langsam entwickelt sich ein Vokabular und eine Kultur der modernen Küche und die heutigen Spitzenköche folgen einer Philosophie, die auf Einfachheit, Ehrlichkeit und Innovation gründet. Ist der Hobbykoch zu Hause bereit, die frischesten Qualitätsprodukte zu verwenden und von den Küchenmeistern zu lernen, welche Zutaten in Geschmack und Textur harmonieren, wird sich der Erfolg von ganz alleine einstellen.

Anna Koor

Adam Ross
Amalia
New York, USA

Adam Ross is Executive Chef at *Amalia*. After graduating from MIT with a degree in physics and a few years spent working in research, he began cooking professionally under celebrity chef Ming Tsai at *Blue Ginger* in Wellesley, Massachusetts. One of his own creations was featured in "East Meets West: the Blue Ginger Cookbook." He went on to work in the kitchens of some of Boston's most renowned restaurants, including four-star luminaries *Rialto* and *No. 9 Park*. He also worked as Sous Chef at *Salts*, which was featured in Travel&Leisure's "Best New American Restaurants" and received four stars from the Boston Herald during his tenure there. Ross has been cooking at *Amalia* since its opening in spring 2007; he stepped into the position of Head Chef six months later. His constantly evolving menu draws inspiration from the diverse cuisines of the Mediterranean and the seasonal, ingredient-driven style called New American.

Adam Ross ist Executive Chef des Restaurants *Amalia*. Er machte zunächst seinen Abschluss in Physik am Massachusetts Institute of Technology und war anschließend einige Jahre in der Forschung tätig, bevor er das Kochen zum Beruf machte und im *Blue Ginger* in Wellesley, Massachusetts unter Starkoch Ming Tsai seine Kochkarriere startete. Eine seiner Kreationen wurde im Kochbuch „East Meets West: the Blue Ginger Cookbook" vorgestellt. Danach stand er in einigen von Bostons renommiertesten Restaurants am Herd, darunter die berühmten Vier-Sterne-Spitzenrestaurants *Rialto* und *No. 9 Park*. Außerdem arbeitete er als Sous Chef im *Salts*, das von der Zeitschrift Travel&Leisure zu einem der „Best New American Restaurants" gekürt wurde und während seiner Anstellung vom Boston Herald vier Sterne erhielt. Ross kocht für das *Amalia* seit dessen Eröffnung im Frühjahr 2007; nach sechs Monaten wurde er zum Küchenchef ernannt. Seine Gerichte entwickeln sich kontinuierlich und er findet Anregungen in den Küchen der Mittelmeerregion und im sogenannten New American-Stil, der auf saisonale Zutaten setzt.

Balsamic-Glazed Short Ribs with Baby Vegetables

Serves 4

2 onions
2 carrots
2 celery stalks
2 apples
2 lb 14 oz short ribs (boneless)
salt, pepper
flour for coating
3 tbs oil
3 whole star-anise
2 cinnamon sticks
4 whole cloves
2 red chili peppers, dried
2 tbs black peppercorns
2 c balsamic vinegar
1 c red wine
4 c chicken stock
4 c white stock

2 lb 3 ½ oz baby vegetables (e.g. carrots, white rutabaga, parsnips, pearl onions, leek)
2 tbs water
2 oz butter
½ bunch of chives

Dice the vegetables and apples. Season short ribs with salt and pepper and coat in flour. Heat oil in a roaster, sear ribs on each side and remove. Now brown the vegetables and apples. Season with salt and pepper, fill the remaining spices into a tea filter and add them to the vegetable mix. Pour vinegar and wine over the mix and simmer gently until thick. Add stock, reboil and add meat. Cover with parchment paper and aluminum foil and leave to stew in a preheated convection oven for 3 ½ hours at 285 °F.

In the meantime, prepare the vegetables for garnish. Wash and cut into bite-sized pieces. Cook the vegetables for the respective cooking time in plenty of salted water until al dente. Rinse in ice-cold water and drain thoroughly. Chop the chives.

Heat 2 tbs of water in a pan, reduce heat and add butter in small amounts to produce a creamy texture. Heat the vegetables in the sauce, add chives and salt to taste.

Remove the meat when ready and keep warm. Strain the stock and reduce to a sauce, making sure to skim off the froth. Cut the meat into 4 pieces of approx. 4 oz and arrange on a plate. Pour a little butter sauce over the vegetables.

Serve with mashed Idaho potatoes.

Rinderrippe mit Balsamico-Glasur und jungem Gemüse

Für 4 Personen

2 Zwiebeln
2 Karotten
2 Stangen Staudensellerie
2 Äpfel
1,3 kg Rinderrippe (ohne Knochen)
Salz, Pfeffer
Mehl zum Wenden
3 EL Öl
3 Sternanis
2 Zimtstangen
4 Nelken
2 getrocknete rote Chilischoten
2 EL schwarze Pfefferkörner
500 ml Balsamico-Essig
250 ml Rotwein
1 l Hühnerbrühe
1 l Kalbsbrühe

1 kg junges Gemüse (z. B. Karotten, weiße Steckrüben, Pastinaken, Silberzwiebeln, Lauch)
2 EL Wasser
60 g Butter
½ Bund Schnittlauch

Gemüse und Äpfel in kleine Würfel schneiden. Die Rinderrippe salzen und pfeffern und in Mehl wenden. In einem Bräter in Öl von allen Seiten anbraten und herausnehmen. Anschließend Gemüse und Äpfel anbräunen. Mit Salz und Pfeffer würzen, die restlichen Gewürze in einem Teefilter zugeben. Essig und Wein zugießen und alles sirupartig einkochen. Mit Brühe auffüllen, erneut aufkochen und das Fleisch zugeben. Mit Backpapier und Alufolie bedeckt im vorgeheizten Backofen bei 140 °C Heißluft ca. 3 ½ Std. schmoren.

In der Zwischenzeit das Gemüse für die Beilage putzen und in mundgerechte Stücke schneiden. In reichlich Salzwasser entsprechend der unterschiedlichen Garzeiten bissfest kochen, in Eiswasser abschrecken und gut abtropfen lassen. Den Schnittlauch in Röllchen schneiden.

In einer Pfanne 2 EL Wasser erhitzen, die Hitze reduzieren und die Butter stückchenweise zugeben, so dass eine cremige Konsistenz entsteht. Gemüse darin heiß werden lassen, Schnittlauch zugeben und mit Salz abschmecken.

Nach Ende der Garzeit das Fleisch herausnehmen und warm halten. Den Sud passieren und zu einer Sauce einkochen, dabei den entstehenden Schaum abschöpfen. Das Fleisch in 4 ca. 120 g schwere Stücke schneiden und jeweils auf einem Teller anrichten. Etwas Gemüse mit der Buttersauce beträufeln.

Servieren Sie dazu Kartoffelpüree von Idaho-Kartoffeln.

Reminiscent of a palace, *Amalia* stands out because of its elaborate Baroque design, giving an impression of wealth and opulence. It was named after Sigmund Freud's mother. *Amalia* consists of a restaurant, bar and lounge, offering space for up to 500 guests on two levels and a total of 26,000 sq. ft. of space. The cuisine has Mediterranean and American influences—the wine list includes wines from cultivation areas in Turkey, Lebanon and Morocco.

Das an einen Palast erinnernde Restaurant besticht durch sein aufwändiges, barockes Design. Es entsteht der Eindruck von Reichtum und Opulenz. Benannt wurde das Lokal nach Sigmund Freuds Mutter. Das *Amalia* besteht aus Restaurant, Bar und Lounge und bietet auf zwei Ebenen und insgesamt 2.400 m² Platz für bis zu 500 Gäste. Die Küche ist mediterran und amerikanisch orientiert – auf der Weinkarte befinden sich auch Weine aus Anbaugebieten der Türkei, des Libanon und Marokkos.

Alexander Lechner
Aux Gazelles
Vienna, Austria

Alexander Lechner is a real all-rounder in the kitchen: whether working in an à-la-carte restaurant or a catering and banquet environment he always learned his craft from scratch. His career began at the *Hotel Scherfler* in Mariazell. Following this, he went on to gain additional culinary skills at different stations in the kitchen as Pastry Chef, Entremetier, Gardemanger, Sous Chef and Head Chef. He worked for *Le Grand Chalet* and *Palace* in Gstaad, the *Grand Hotel* in Vienna as well as restaurants such as *Danieli, Noodles, Stern* and *Theatercafe* in Vienna, among others. The young father has built up a varied repertoire of many different recipes with Viennese, Scandinavian, and Arab being his favorite cuisines. He celebrates his third year at *Aux Gazelles* in 2008.

Alexander Lechner ist ein Allrounder in der Küche: Ob à la Carte, im Bankett- oder auch im Catering-Betrieb, er hat sein Handwerk von der Pike auf gelernt. Begonnen hat seine Karriere im *Hotel Scherfler* in Mariazell. Im Anschluss daran erweiterte er seine Kenntnisse in verschiedenen Stationen als Patissier, Entremetier, Gardemanger, Sous Chef und Küchenchef. Unter anderem war er in den Hotels *Le Grand Chalet* und *Palace* in Gstaad, im *Grand Hotel*, Wien, sowie den Restaurants *Danieli, Noodles, Stern* und *Theatercafe* in Wien tätig. Der junge Familienvater beherrscht heute ein breit gefächertes Repertoire verschiedenster Stile, wobei seine Vorlieben bei der Wiener Küche, der Skandinavischen Küche und der Arabischen Küche liegen. Im *Aux Gazelles* feiert er im Jahre 2008 sein dreijähriges Firmenjubiläum.

Poulet au Citron de la Maison

Poulet au Citron de la Maison

Serves 2

1 chicken (approx. 3 lb)
3 tbs olive oil
1 tsp turmeric
1 tsp ground ginger
½ preserved lemon
10 pitted green olives
juice from 3 lemons
½ tsp saffron strands
1 pinch sweet paprika powder
1 tsp ground cumin
salt, pepper
½ bunch cilantro
1 tbs sesame seeds

Carefully separate chicken breasts from the bone leaving on the skin and remove thighs. Mix olive oil, 1 pinch of turmeric and the ground ginger in a bowl, add the meat, cover and allow to marinate for at least 6 hours in the refrigerator. Finely chop the preserved lemon and cut the olives into small pieces.

Then place the chicken thighs next to one another in a pot or tajine, add the lemon juice, spices, olives and preserved lemon and salt to taste. Cover the chicken thighs with water. Put in a preheated convection oven at 340 °F for approx. 45–50 min.

The meat is ready when it can easily be pulled from the bone. 10 min. before the end of cooking time place the chicken breasts in a non-stick pan and fry them, skin side down, until crispy brown. Season with salt and pepper and place them on the chicken thighs, meat side down. Put in the oven for another 5 min.

Wash and dry the cilantro, then remove the leaves from the stems and chop finely. Arrange the chicken on a plate or serve it in the tajine, sprinkle with sesame seeds and top with chopped cilantro.

Für 2 Personen

1 Huhn (ca. 1,4 kg)
3 EL Olivenöl
1 TL Kurkuma
1 TL gemahlener Ingwer
½ konfierte Zitrone
10 entsteinte, grüne Oliven
Saft von 3 Zitronen
½ TL Safranfäden
1 Prise edelsüßes Paprikapulver
1 TL gemahlener Kreuzkümmel
Salz, Pfeffer
½ Bund Koriander
1 EL Sesam

Die Hühnerbrüste mit der Haut von den Knochen trennen und die Schenkel auslösen. Olivenöl mit 1 Prise Kurkuma und dem Ingwer vermischen, abdecken und das Fleisch darin mindestens 6 Std. im Kühlschrank marinieren. Die konfierte Zitrone fein hacken. Die Oliven klein schneiden.

Anschließend die Schenkel in einer hohen Pfanne oder einer Tajine nebeneinander legen und mit dem Zitronensaft, Gewürzen, Oliven und Zitronenkonfit vermischen und salzen. Mit so viel Wasser auffüllen, dass die Schenkel knapp bedeckt sind. Im vorgeheizten Backofen bei 170 °C Heißluft ca. 45 – 50 Min. garen.

Das Fleisch ist fertig, wenn es sich einfach vom Knochen lösen lässt. 10 Min. vor Ende der Garzeit die Hühnerbrüste in einer beschichteten Pfanne auf der Hautseite knusprig anbraten, mit Salz und Pfeffer würzen und mit der Fleischseite auf die Schenkel legen. Im Backofen in ca. 5 Min. fertig braten.

Den Koriander waschen, trocken schütteln, Blätter abzupfen und fein hacken. Das Geflügel in der Tajine oder auf Tellern angerichtet mit Sesam und gehacktem Koriander bestreut servieren.

The *Aux Gazelles* combines several different worlds on more than 17.000 sq. ft.: in addition to the nightclub, oyster bar, brasserie, bazaar and deli, it boasts a Moroccan hammam with an adjoining tea salon for relaxation. The kitchen of the restaurant, which opened in 2002, produces a diverse range of North African and French delicacies. The caviar and oyster bar offers a selection of twelve brands of champagne. Three days a week, the Oriental atmosphere of the place is underscored by exotic sounds in the nightclub.

Das *Aux Gazelles* vereint auf mehr als 1.600 m² gleich mehrere Welten: Neben Nachtklub, Austernbar, Brasserie, Basar und Deli gibt es hier einen marokkanischen Hamam mit angrenzendem Teesalon zum Entspannen. Die Küche des 2002 eröffneten Lokals kreiert ein vielfältiges Angebot an nordafrikanischen und französischen Köstlichkeiten. An der Kaviar- und Austernbar stehen zwölf Champagnersorten zur Auswahl. Die orientalische Atmosphäre wird im Nachtklub an drei Tagen pro Woche von exotischen Sounds untermalt.

Robbie Lewis
bacar
San Francisco, USA

Robbie Lewis spent his childhood in Little Rock, Arkansas before moving to San Francisco in 1992 to embark on a culinary career. For the last 15 years he has cooked in many of the Bay Area's most revered kitchens alongside renowned chefs and gained an appreciation for fine cuisine. While at the California Culinary Academy he worked nights at *Boulevard* where a chance meeting with acclaimed chef Traci Des Jardins initiated an enduring professional friendship that landed him in the kitchen at *Rubicon* where Des Jardins was the Opening Chef. He continued to evolve by working in restaurants in France, Italy, and Spain before taking on the roles of Opening Sous Chef at the chic Mediterranean restaurant *42 Degrees*, and the award-winning Woodside establishment, *The Village Pub*. After a brief stint at *Chez Panisse* he was named Executive Chef at Traci Des Jardins' *Jardinière* in 2002. Taking the reins as Executive Chef of *bacar*, Lewis creates delicious, beautifully executed dishes designed to pair with the restaurant's impressive 1,200-bottle wine collection.

Robbie Lewis wuchs in Little Rock, Arkansas auf und zog 1992 nach San Francisco, wo seine Kochkarriere begann. Seit 15 Jahren kocht er in vielen renommierten Küchen der Bay Area neben namhaften Köchen und lernte dabei die Haute Cuisine schätzen. Während seiner Zeit an der California Culinary Academy arbeitete er nachts im Restaurant *Boulevard*. Dort traf er zufällig auf die gefeierte Köchin Traci Des Jardins – der Beginn einer langen beruflichen Freundschaft, die Lewis in die Küche des *Rubicon* brachte, wo Des Jardins Opening Chef war. Anstellungen in Restaurants in Frankreich, Italien und Spanien trugen zu seiner weiteren Entwicklung bei. Lewis wurde schließlich Opening Sous Chef im eleganten, auf mediterrane Küche spezialisierten Restaurant *42 Degrees* und im preisgekrönten *The Village Pub* in Woodside. Nach einem kurzen Gastspiel im *Chez Panisse* wurde er 2002 zum Executive Chef in Traci Des Jardins' Restaurant *Jardinière* ernannt. Nun hat er im *bacar* als Executive Chef das Zepter in der Hand und kreiert köstliche, ansprechend angerichtete Speisen, die mit der beeindruckenden, 1200 Flaschen umfassenden Weinsammlung des Restaurants harmonieren sollen.

Herbed Rack of Lamb with Tomato Braised Shelled Beans and Moroccan Spiced Eggplants

Serves 6

6 ½ oz white giant beans, dried
2 onions
4 cloves of garlic
3.3 oz carrots
3.3 oz celery
3.3 oz leek
2 oranges
4 tomatoes
olive oil for the casserole
1 oz bacon, diced
1 tbs tomato puree
1 bunch of thyme
2 tbs Raz el Hanout
salt
4 c chicken stock
3 Japanese eggplants
¼ c 3 tsp sherry vinegar
¼ c 3 tsp honey
pepper
½ bunch of parsley
3 sprigs of mint
3 lamb racks (13.3 oz each)
1 bunch of watercress
6 ½ oz French Feta cheese

Soak beans overnight in plenty of cold water. Peel and dice onions and garlic. Wash, peel and dice the vegetables. Peel the oranges, remove the white skin, cut in half and slice. Wash and dice tomatoes.

Heat olive oil in a casserole, and brown the onions and diced bacon. Add the vegetables and garlic and brown at medium heat. Add tomato puree, drained beans, oranges, tomatoes and 4 sprigs of thyme. Season with 1 tbs of Raz el Hanout and salt, pour chicken stock over the mix, bring to boil and cover, cook at low heat until the beans are tender. Then remove cover and reduce until viscid. Wash the eggplants, cut into thin stripes, season with salt and leave to brew for about 30 min. Heat sherry vinegar and honey in a casserole. Season with the remaining Raz el Hanout, salt and pepper. Roast the eggplants in olive oil until tender, season with salt and pepper. Drain on paper towels and allow to cool in the marinade. Wash the herbs and shake off excess water, pluck off and chop the leaves. Season racks of lamb with salt and pepper and sear in olive oil, 5–6 min. each side until slightly brown. Remove racks of lamb, coat in chopped herbs and keep warm for 10 min. Clean, wash and spin dry the watercress.

Season beans again to taste, add some olive oil and arrange on six plates. Cut racks of lamb into chops and place two onto the beans on each plate. Add watercress to eggplants, stir and arrange on the chops. Sprinkle Feta cheese on top and serve.

Kräuterlammkarrees mit in Tomaten geschmorten Bohnen und marokkanisch gewürzten Auberginen

Für 6 Personen

200 g getrocknete weiße Riesenbohnen
2 Zwiebeln
4 Knoblauchzehen
100 g Karotten
100 g Staudensellerie
100 g Lauch
2 Orangen
4 Tomaten
Olivenöl zum Braten
30 g Schinkenwürfel
1 EL Tomatenmark
1 Bund Thymian
2 EL Raz el Hanout
Salz
1 l Hühnerbrühe
3 japanische Auberginen
75 ml Sherry-Essig
75 ml Honig
Pfeffer
½ Bund glatte Petersilie
3 Stängel Minze
3 Lammkarrees (à 400 g)
1 Bund Brunnenkresse
200 g französischer Fetakäse

Die Bohnen über Nacht in reichlich kaltem Wasser einweichen. Zwiebeln und Knoblauch schälen und fein würfeln. Gemüse putzen, schälen und in kleine Würfel schneiden. Orangen samt der weißen Haut schälen, halbieren und in Scheiben schneiden. Tomaten waschen und würfeln.

In einem Topf Olivenöl erhitzen, Zwiebeln und Schinkenwürfel darin anbraten. Gemüse und Knoblauch zugeben und bei mittlerer Hitze ebenfalls anbraten. Tomatenmark, abgetropfte Bohnen, Orangen, Tomaten und 4 Thymianzweige zugeben. Mit 1 EL Raz el Hanout und Salz würzen, Hühnerbrühe zugießen, aufkochen und zugedeckt bei geringer Hitze garen, bis die Bohnen weich sind. Anschließend ohne Deckel auf eine sämige Konsistenz einkochen. Auberginen putzen, in dünne Streifen schneiden, salzen und ca. 30 Min. ziehen lassen. In einem Topf Sherry-Essig und Honig erwärmen. Mit dem restlichen Raz el Hanout, Salz und Pfeffer würzen. Die Auberginen in Olivenöl braten, bis sie weich sind, salzen und pfeffern. Auf Küchenpapier abtropfen und in der Marinade abkühlen lassen. Die Kräuter waschen, trocken schütteln, Blätter abzupfen und fein hacken. Die Lammkarrees mit Salz und Pfeffer würzen und in Olivenöl von jeder Seite ca. 5 – 6 Min. braten, bis sie leicht gebräunt sind. Die Lammkarrees herausnehmen, in den gehackten Kräutern wenden und für 10 Min. warm halten. Die Brunnenkresse putzen, waschen und trocken schleudern.

Zum Anrichten die Bohnen nochmals abschmecken, mit Olivenöl verfeinern und auf sechs Tellern anrichten. Die Lammkarrees in einzelne Koteletts zerteilen und jeweils 2 auf die Bohnen geben. Brunnenkresse mit den Auberginen mischen und auf die Koteletts geben. Fetakäse darüber bröseln und servieren.

This elegantly furnished restaurant in a renovated brick building offers Northern Californian cuisine with a Mediterranean touch. Its large wine selection simultaneously serves as a design element: the wine rack with its multitude of bottles behind a glass front extends from the lounge on the lower level all the way to the gallery. Meals are served on three levels with space for 150 guests. Large round arches as well as skylights provide lots of daylight. Jazz bands perform there at weekends.

Dieses stilvoll eingerichtete Restaurant in einem renovierten Backsteingebäude bietet nordkalifornische Küche mit mediterranem Einschlag. Die große Weinauswahl ist zugleich Design-Element: Das Weinregal mit zahlreichen Flaschen hinter einer Glasfront erstreckt sich von der Lounge im Untergeschoss bis zur Galerie. Auf drei Ebenen kann gespeist werden, 150 Gäste finden hier Platz. Große Rundbogen- sowie Dachfenster sorgen für viel Tageslicht. An Wochenenden treten auch Jazzbands auf.

Cass Titcombe
Canteen
London, UK

Cass Titcombe is *Canteen's* Executive Chef and co-founder (pictured far right). He cut his teeth in West Country restaurants before moving to London to head up the kitchens of *Daphne's* and *The Collection*. He later ran the kitchen at the *Real Eating Company* in Brighton, a much revered exercise in quality British dining where he was able to apply his own ethos to a project. Quality of produce and its provenance has always been of utmost importance to Titcombe. As a child he lived and grew up in Wales; his parents had a small holding where they produced everything, grew vegetables and raised livestock. It is the belief of Titcombe and his partners Dominic Lake and Patrick Malone in the potential of British cuisine, honestly prepared food and the importance of food provenance that drives the *Canteen* kitchen.

Cass Titcombe (Foto ganz rechts) ist Executive Chef und Mitbegründer des Restaurants *Canteen*. Er verdiente sich seine Sporen in Restaurants im Südwesten Englands, bevor er nach London übersiedelte, wo er im *Daphne's* und im *The Collection* für die Küche verantwortlich war. Später übernahm er die Leitung der Küche im Restaurant *Real Eating Company* in Brighton – ein fabelhaftes Training in Bezug auf britische Qualitätsgastronomie – und konnte seine eigenen Ideen und Vorstellungen in ein Projekt einbringen. Die Qualität der Produkte und ihre Herkunft waren für Titcombe schon immer äußerst wichtig. Er verbrachte seine Kindheit in Wales, wo seine Eltern ein kleines Stück Land besaßen und alles selbst produzierten: Gemüse anbauten und Vieh züchteten. Der Glaube Titcombes und seiner Partner Dominic Lake und Patrick Malone an das Potential der britischen Küche, einfach zubereitete Gerichte und die Bedeutung der Herkunft der Zutaten ist die Triebfeder der *Canteen*-Küche.

Steak and Kidney Pie

Serves 8

6 ½ oz ox kidneys
1 onion
3 cloves of garlic
2 celery stalks
1 carrot
1 small leek
2 tsp dried Porcini mushrooms
1 lb 2 oz beef (from the leg)
salt, black pepper
allspice
flour for coating
2 tbs oil
¾ c Guinness or other beer
2 c beef stock
1 tbs Worcester sauce
2 bay leaves
5 sprigs of thyme
1 lb 2 oz fresh pastry
flour for work surface
butter to grease the pie tin
1 egg

Rinse the kidneys in plenty of water. Peel and dice onions and garlic. Wash celery and carrot and dice as well. Wash and slice leek, cut Porcini mushrooms into small pieces. Coarsely dice beef, season with salt, pepper and allspice. Then coat in flour. Heat oil in a roaster, sear beef on all sides, then remove. Add the vegetables and onion and roast for about 3 min. Add meat, garlic, beer, stock, Worcester sauce, dried mushrooms, bay leaves and 5 sprigs of thyme, bring to a boil, cover and cook in a preheated convection oven at 250 °F for about 90 min.

Clean the kidneys, dice and season with pepper, allspice and salt. Add to the beef, stir and cook for another 30 min. When cooking time is up, the meat should be tender but not fall apart. Strain the mix, keep the liquid, simmer and reduce liquid to half and season to taste. Set sauce and beef aside to cool.

In the meantime, roll the pastry on a floured surface and cut two circles the size of the pie tin. Grease bottom and sides of the pie tin and line with one pastry circle. Pour the filling in and cover with the second pastry shell. Seal the edges with a fork. Whisk the egg and brush on pastry. Poke a few holes into the pastry shell with a fork to allow steam to escape. Bake in a preheated convection oven at 350 °F for about 25–30 min.

Cut the pie into pieces and serve with mashed potatoes, buttered green vegetables and the warm sauce.

Rindfleisch-Nieren-Pastete

Für 8 Personen

200 g Ochsennieren
1 Zwiebel
3 Knoblauchzehen
2 Stangen Staudensellerie
1 Karotte
1 kleine Stange Lauch
10 g getrocknete Steinpilze
500 g Rindfleisch (aus der Keule)
Salz, schwarzer Pfeffer
Nelkenpfeffer
Mehl zum Wenden
2 EL Öl
200 ml Guinness oder anderes Bier
500 ml Rinderbrühe
1 EL Worcester-Sauce
2 Lorbeerblätter
5 Zweige Thymian
500 g frischen Blätterteig
Mehl zum Bearbeiten
Butter zum Einfetten
1 Ei

Die Nieren reichlich wässern. Zwiebel und Knoblauchzehen schälen, alles fein würfeln. Staudensellerie und Karotte putzen und ebenfalls in kleine Würfel schneiden. Den geputzten Lauch in Scheiben, die Steinpilze klein schneiden. Das Rindfleisch grob würfeln, mit Salz, Pfeffer und reichlich Nelkenpfeffer würzen. Anschließend in Mehl wenden. Öl in einem Bräter erhitzen, das Rindfleisch darin rundherum anbraten, anschließend herausnehmen. Gemüse und Zwiebel zugeben und ca. 3 Min. anbraten. Fleisch, Knoblauch, Bier, Brühe, Worcester-Sauce, getrocknete Pilze, Lorbeerblätter und 5 Zweige Thymian zugeben, alles aufkochen und zugedeckt im vorgeheizten Backofen bei 120 °C Heißluft ca. 90 Min. garen.

Die Nieren säubern, in kleine Würfel schneiden und mit Pfeffer und Nelkenpfeffer sowie Salz würzen. Unter das Rindfleisch mischen und weitere 30 Min. garen. Nach Ende der Garzeit sollte das Fleisch zart sein, jedoch nicht zusammenfallen. Das Gulasch passieren, die aufgefangene Flüssigkeit auf die Hälfte reduzieren und abschmecken. Sauce und das passierte Fleisch abkühlen lassen.

Währenddessen den Blätterteig auf einer bemehlten Arbeitsfläche ausrollen und 2 Teigkreise passend für die Pastetenform zurechtschneiden. Boden und Rand der Form fetten und mit einem Teigkreis auslegen. Die Füllung darauf verteilen, den zweiten Blätterteigkreis als Deckel auflegen und den Rand mit einer Gabel andrücken. Das Ei verquirlen und den Blätterteig damit bestreichen. Mit einer Gabel einige Löcher in den Blätterteigdeckel stechen, damit der Dampf entweichen kann. Im vorgeheizten Backofen bei 175 °C Heißluft ca. 25 – 30 Min. backen.

Die Pastete in Stücke schneiden und mit Kartoffelpüree, gebuttertem Grüngemüse und der erwärmten Sauce servieren.

Opened in 2005, *Canteen* Spitalfields serves modern British cuisine at fair prices. They even serve breakfast all day. A winner of numerous awards for both its food and its design, this restaurant places much value on national, high-quality produce and great British workmanship. The perfectly designed, simple interior is inspired by public establishments. In June 2007, the popular and much-frequented restaurant opened a branch at the Royal Festival Hall and in October 2008 *Canteen* Baker Street will open. Since opening in Spitalfields in 2005 *Canteen* has won several awards in recognition of its great modern British menu such as The Good Food Guide's Best London Restaurant 2007 and the Observer Food Monthly's Best UK Restaurant 2007.

2005 eröffnet, wird hier moderne britische Küche zu fairen Preisen serviert. Frühstück gibt es sogar ganztägig. Das sowohl für sein Essen als auch für sein Design mehrfach preisgekrönte Lokal legt viel Wert auf nationale, hochwertige Produkte und deren solide Verarbeitung. Das formvollendete, schlichte Interieur orientiert sich an öffentlichen Einrichtungen. Seit Juni 2007 hat das beliebte und gut besuchte Lokal einen Ableger in der Royal Festival Hall und im Oktober 2008 wird *Canteen* Baker Street eröffnet. Seit seiner Eröffnung im Londoner Stadtteil Spitalfields im Jahr 2005 hat das *Canteen* mehrere Auszeichnungen in Anerkennung seiner großartigen und modernen britischen Küche erhalten, darunter die Titel Best London Restaurant 2007 (The Good Food Guide) und Best UK Restaurant 2007 (Observer Food Monthly).

Bruno Ballistreri
Centrale Restaurant Lounge
Venice, Italy

Bruno Ballistreri comes from Medolla and attended the Federazione Italiana di Cuochi at an early age. His impressive career includes positions at the following restaurants: *Castello, Fini, Don Chisciotte, Grand Hotel Rocca Pendice, Il Genacolo* and *Hotel Villa Quaranta*. He has been an expert on medieval cuisine for about 20 years and has been acting as an expert consultant for the restaurant trade since the late 80s. Over the past two years he has captured the imagination of locals and visitors alike with traditional recipes of Venetian cuisine in the original neo-renaissance style at the *Centrale*. He has received many accolades and awards for his achievements such as the Collegio Cocorum in 1998 as well as becoming first Treasurer and eventually President of the Italian Association of Chefs in 2000.

Der aus Medolla stammende Bruno Ballistreri trat schon in jungen Jahren in die Federazione Italiana di Cuochi ein. Seine beeindrucken-de Laufbahn umfasst unter anderem Stationen in den folgenden Restaurants Italiens: *Castello, Fini, Don Chisciotte, Grand Hotel Rocca Pendice, Il Genacolo* und *Hotel Villa Quaranta*. Seit etwa 20 Jahren ist er Spezialist für die Küche des Mittelalters, und seit Ende der 80er Jahre nimmt er verschiedene Beratertätigkeiten im Restaurantgewerbe wahr. Im *Centrale* begeistert er seit zwei Jahren Ortsansässige wie Besucher mit Rezepten der originalen venezianischen Küche, präsentiert in einem Restaurant im unverfälschten Neorenaissance-Stil. Seine Leistungen wurden mit mehreren Auszeichnungen gewürdigt: Collegio Cocorum (1998) sowie die Ernennung zunächst zum Schatzmeister und 2000 zum Vorsitzenden des Verbandes Italienischer Küchenchefs.

Praline of Salmon and Turbot in an Almond Crust

Serves 4

10 oz turbot filet
3.3 oz white bread
½ c 2 tbs cream
1 egg white (medium size)
salt, pepper
6 ½ oz salmon filet
3.3 oz fresh spinach
3.3 oz sliced almonds
olive oil for frying
1 yellow pepper
3 tbs olive oil
pink pepper berries

Wash the turbot filets and pat dry. Chop bread coarsely and puree together with the filets, cream and egg white. Season with salt and pepper and place in the fridge. Wash the salmon filets and cut into four equal pieces.

Wash spinach, remove stems and blanch in boiling salted water for 1–2 seconds. Rinse in ice-cold water, squeeze gently and place on 4 sheets of plastic wrap, allowing the edges to slightly overlap. Pat dry with paper towels. Spread a thin layer of filling on each piece of salmon, then place on the spinach leaves, wrap and roll into small balls.

Coat the little balls with the remaining filling and cover with sliced almonds. Place on a baking tray covered with parchment paper and bake in a preheated convection oven at 355 °F for approx. 5–6 min. until the little balls are quite firm. Fry in plenty of olive oil until the almonds are golden brown and keep warm.

For the sauce, wash the pepper, cut into quarters, remove seeds and white inner skins. Grill skin side up at 390 °F for approx. 5–6 min. Remove, cover with a moist cloth, leave to cool slightly and remove the skin. Add olive oil and puree to create a creamy sauce, reheat and season to taste.

Cut the little balls into slices, garnish with pink pepper berries and serve with the pepper sauce.

Praliné von Lachs und Steinbutt in Mandelkruste

Für 4 Personen

300 g Steinbuttfilet
100 g Weißbrot
150 ml Sahne
1 Eiweiß (Größe M)
Salz, Pfeffer
200 g Lachsfilet
100 g frischer Spinat
100 g gehobelte Mandeln
Olivenöl zum Ausbacken
1 gelbe Paprikaschote
3 EL Olivenöl
rosa Pfefferbeeren

Die Steinbuttfilets waschen und trocken tupfen. Weißbrot grob zerkleinern und zusammen mit den Filets, Sahne und Eiweiß pürieren. Mit Salz und Pfeffer würzen und kalt stellen. Lachsfilets waschen und in vier gleichmäßige Stücke schneiden.

Den Spinat ebenfalls waschen, die Stiele entfernen und in kochendem Salzwasser für 1 – 2 Sek. blanchieren. Anschließend in Eiswasser abschrecken, leicht ausdrücken und leicht überlappend auf 4 Bögen Frischhaltefolie legen. Mit Küchenpapier trocken tupfen. Jedes Lachsstück dünn mit etwas Farce bestreichen, auf die Spinatblätter legen, einwickeln und zu Bällchen formen.

Die Bällchen mit der restlichen Farce umhüllen und in den gehobelten Mandeln wälzen. Auf ein mit Backpapier ausgelegtes Blech setzen und im vorgeheizten Backofen bei 180 °C Heißluft ca. 5 – 6 Min. backen, bis die Bällchen fest sind. Anschließend in reichlich Olivenöl ausbacken, bis die Mandelblättchen goldbraun sind, anschließend warm halten.

Für die Sauce die Paprika waschen, vierteln, Kerne und weiße Innenhäute entfernen. Unter dem Backofengrill bei 200 °C mit der Hautseite nach oben ca. 5 – 6 Min. grillen. Herausnehmen, mit einem feuchten Tuch bedecken, leicht abkühlen lassen und die Haut abziehen. Mit Olivenöl zu einer sämigen Sauce pürieren, nochmals erwärmen und abschmecken.

Die Bällchen in Scheiben schneiden, mit rosa Pfefferbeeren garnieren und mit der Paprikasauce servieren.

Located in a Venetian palace from the second half of the 16th Century—very close to St. Mark's Square—this restaurant offers dining of the stylish and glamorous kind. Traditional Venetian dishes centering on meat and fish are served in its atmospheric rooms. Lobster also plays a main role on the menu. The illuminated bar contrasts with the old brick walls of the restaurant and even the restroom is a visual highlight. Candlelight and soft music underscore the overall romantic ambience.

In einem venezianischen Palast aus der zweiten Hälfte des 16. Jahrhunderts gelegen, wird hier – ganz nah am Markusplatz – vornehm und glamourös gespeist. In stimmungsvollem Ambiente werden traditionell venezianische Gerichte rund um Fleisch und Fisch serviert. Auch Hummer spielt eine Hauptrolle auf der Speisekarte. Die beleuchtete Bar kontrastiert mit den alten Backsteinwänden, und selbst die Toilette ist ein optisches Highlight. Kerzenschein und sanfte Musik untermalen das romantische Ambiente.

Kong Khai Meng
The China House
Bangkok, Thailand

Kong Khai Meng heads the culinary team as Resident Chef of the newly reopened *The China House* at *The Oriental Hotel*, Bangkok and is one of Consultant Chef Jereme Leung's brightest protégés. His extensive experience in both Hong Kong and Shanghai has trained him in all aspects of Chinese cooking, however at *The China House* his menu features a combination of classic Cantonese cuisine. Born in Singapore, his career has taken him across Asia and the Middle East with luxury hotel groups such as the *Four Seasons* and *Mandarin Oriental*. As Chinese Executive Chef at *Le Méridien Hotel* in Dubai from 2003 to 2005 his reputation earned him accolades in the local media for his innovative approach to traditional ethnic Asian cuisine. Before joining *The China House*, Kong Khai Meng worked at the highly praised *Whampoa Club*, Shanghai where he honed his talents in creating both traditional and fine Shanghai cuisine with a modern touch, selecting ingredients from other provinces of China to introduce new experiences to the taste buds.

Kong Khai Meng leitet als Resident Chef das Küchenteam des vor Kurzem wiedereröffneten *The China House* im *Oriental Hotel* in Bangkok und gilt als einer der begabtesten Protegés des Consultant Chefs Jereme Leung. Durch seine umfangreichen Erfahrungen in Hongkong und Schanghai ist er in allen Bereichen der chinesischen Küche ausgebildet. Im *The China House* umfasst seine Speisekarte eine Auswahl klassischer kantonesischer Gerichte. In Singapur geboren, führte ihn seine Karriere quer durch Asien und den Nahen Osten, in Luxushotelgruppen wie das *Four Seasons* und das *Mandarin Oriental*. Von 2003 bis 2005 war Kong Khai Meng chinesischer Executive Chef im *Le Méridien Hotel* in Dubai, wo er für seine innovative Interpretation der traditionellen und ursprünglichen asiatischen Küche viel Lob in den lokalen Medien erntete. Bevor er zum *The China House* kam, stand Kong Khai Meng im hochgelobten *Whampoa Club* in Shanghai am Herd. Dort verfeinerte er sein Können im Kreieren traditioneller Gerichte sowie gehobener Speisen der Schanghai-Küche mit moderner Note, indem er Zutaten aus anderen Provinzen Chinas verwendete, um den Geschmacksknospen seiner Gäste Neues zu bieten.

Wok-seared Tiger Prawns with Kumquat Sauce

Serves 4

For the bean paste
1 ½ oz garlic
1 ½ oz shallots
1 oz red chili peppers
1 oz dried red chili peppers
¾ oz chicken powder
2 ½ oz sugar
6 ½ oz brown bean paste

For the kumquat sauce
¾ oz red chili peppers
8.3 oz kumquats, untreated
12 tiger prawns (approx. 2 lb 3 ½ oz)
cornstarch for coating
1 c oil
⅓ c lemon juice
1 c plum paste
2 ½ oz bean paste, warm
¼ oz salt

For the beanpaste, peel and dice garlic and shallots. Wash the fresh chili peppers, remove the seeds and the inner white skins. Cut into small pieces, together with the dried chili peppers. Mix with other ingredients for the bean paste in a pot, stir and cook on a low heat for approx. 20 min. and keep warm.

For the kumquat sauce, wash the chili peppers, remove the seeds and white inner skins and cut into strips. Wash the kumquats in hot water, slice and remove seeds.

Wash prawns, pat dry, peel, cut along the back and remove the intestinal tracts. Coat in cornstarch. Heat oil in the wok and fry prawns for approx. 3 min. Remove and drain on paper towels.

Remove the remaining oil apart from a small amount and reheat the wok; add kumquats, lemon juice, plum paste, strips of chili pepper, stir in 2 ½ oz of the prepared warm bean paste, season with salt and cook for approx. 10 min. Add the tiger prawns and warm through. Arrange and serve immediately.

Im Wok gebratene Riesengarnelen mit Kumquat-Sauce

Für 4 Personen

Bohnenpaste
50 g Knoblauch
50 g Schalotte
25 g rote Chilischote
25 g getrocknete rote Chilischote
20 g Hühnerpulver
80 g Zucker
200 g braune Bohnenpaste

Kumquat-Sauce
20 g rote Chilischote
250 g unbehandelte Kumquats
12 Riesengarnelen (ca. 1 kg)
Speisestärke zum Wenden
250 ml Öl
80 ml Zitronensaft
250 g Pflaumenpaste
80 g warme Bohnenpaste
8 g Salz

Für die Bohnenpaste Knoblauch und Schalotte schälen und würfeln. Frische Chilischote waschen, Kerne und weiße Innenhäute entfernen und zusammen mit der getrockneten klein schneiden. In einem Topf alles mit den restlichen Zutaten für die Bohnenpaste verrühren, bei geringer Hitze ca. 20 Min. kochen und warm halten.

Für die Kumquat-Sauce die Chilischote waschen, Kerne und weiße Innenhäute entfernen und in Streifen schneiden. Die Kumquats heiß abwaschen, in Scheiben schneiden und entkernen.

Die Garnelen waschen, trocken tupfen, schälen, am Rückgrat aufschneiden und den Darmfaden entfernen. Anschließend in Speisestärke wenden. Das Öl im Wok erhitzen und die Garnelen darin ca. 3 Min. ausbacken. Herausnehmen und auf Küchenpapier abtropfen lassen.

Das Öl bis auf einen kleinen Rest entfernen und diesen erneut erhitzen. Kumquats, Zitronensaft, Pflaumenpaste, Chilistreifen zugeben, 80 g der vorbereiteten warmen Bohnenpaste unterrühren, mit dem Salz würzen und alles ca. 10 Min. kochen. Dann die Riesengarnelen wieder zugeben und heiß werden lassen. Sofort anrichten und servieren.

Located in the two-storey colonial building of Bangkok's famed *Oriental Hotel* a meticulous makeover has transformed the Cantonese restaurant into an avant-garde dining experience combining the opulence of 1930s Shanghai with contemporary details in lighting, color, and style. Diners are greeted by 100 overhead red lanterns leading to a red chamber surrounded by screens and columns clad in high gloss Macassar ebony. Signature dishes are prepared from an external show kitchen and opium-bed banquettes provide intimate privacy.

Das Restaurant befindet sich im zweistöckigen Kolonialbau des berühmten *Oriental Hotel* in Bangkok. Dank einer sorgfältigen und grundlegenden Umgestaltung bietet das kantonesische Restaurant nun den Rahmen für ein avantgardistisches Gastronomieerlebnis – der Wohlstand des Schanghai der 30er Jahre vereint sich mit zeitgenössischen Details in Beleuchtung, Farbe und Stil. 100 rote Laternen an der Decke empfangen die Gäste und führen sie in einen roten Saal, der von Paravents und mit hochglänzenden Makassa-Ebenholz verkleideten Säulen umgeben ist. Vorzeigegerichte des Restaurants werden in einer separaten, einsehbaren Küche zubereitet; Bänke, die an Opiumbetten erinnern, schaffen eine intime Atmosphäre.

Michael Kempf
FACIL Restaurant
Berlin, Germany

Michael Kempf was born in Sigmaringen, Germany and began his apprenticeship at *Hotel Kleber-Post* in Saulgau in 1993. He quickly rose through the ranks of the culinary profession, nurturing his cooking techniques in the kitchens of various renowned restaurants. At the *Wald- und Schlosshotel Friedrichsruhe* he was Poissonnier under Grand Chef Lothar Eiermann from 1997 to 1999. He then joined Restaurant *Fischerzunft Schaffhausen* in Switzerland headed by André Jaeger as Gardemanger, Entremetier, Saucier; and in 2001 he became Saucier and Entremetier at *Restaurant Dieter Mueller* in Bergisch Gladbach. In April 2003 he was announced Chef de Cuisine at *Facil* in the *Mandala Hotel*, Berlin, which he regards as one of Germany's most exciting gourmet restaurants.

Michael Kempf wurde in Sigmaringen geboren und begann 1993 seine Ausbildung im *Hotel Kleber-Post* in Saulgau. Schnell arbeitete er sich nach ganz oben; pflegte und verbesserte seine Kochtechniken in den Küchen verschiedener renommierter Restaurants. Von 1997 bis 1999 war Kempf Poissonnier im *Wald- und Schlosshotel Friedrichsruhe* unter Küchenchef Lothar Eiermann. Danach zog es ihn in die Schweiz ins von André Jaeger geleitete Restaurant *Fischerzunft Schaffhausen*, wo er als Gardemanger, Entremetier und Saucier tätig war. 2001 wurde er Saucier und Entremetier im *Restaurant Dieter Müller* in Bergisch Gladbach. Im April 2003 folgte schließlich die Ernennung zum Küchenchef des *Facil* im *Mandala Hotel* in Berlin – ein Restaurant, das seiner Meinung nach zu den aufregendsten Gourmettempeln Deutschlands zählt.

Arctic Cod on a Bell Pepper Compote with Charcoal Oil and Amalfi Lemon

Serves 4

½ c 2 tbs vegetable oil
1 ½ oz charcoal
5 red bell peppers
2 shallots
1 clove of garlic
1 ½ oz chorizo
3 tbs olive oil
1 lemon, untreated
¼ tsp smoked paprika powder
¼ tsp ground cumin
1 bay leaf
sea salt, pepper
¼ tsp harissa
juice of ½ marinated Amalfi lemon
4 Arctic cod filets, scaled with skin (5 oz each)
1 tbs butter
1 sprig of thyme
1 tbs capers
olive oil for frying

Heat the oil to 140 °F, break the charcoal into smaller pieces and cover with the heated oil. Cover and set aside for approx. 24 hours, then strain.

Wash the bell peppers, skin with a peeler and clean. Puree skins and removed flesh and strain through a fine cloth. Cut the bell peppers into diamond shapes. Peel shallots and garlic. Together with the chorizo, finely dice and brown in 1 tbs of olive oil. Add pepper diamonds and sauté with the other ingredients. Add paprika powder, cumin, bay leaf and finely grated lemon zest and roast. Season with salt, pepper, harissa and lemon juice. Then cook pepper diamonds for approx. 10 min until firm to bite. Add bell pepper juice, bring to a boil, reduce liquid to desired consistency and season to taste.

Wash the fish filets and pat dry. Heat the remaining olive oil and gently sear skin-side down until crispy. Turn over, add butter and sprig of thyme and cook on a medium heat for approx. 5 min. Season with salt.

Fry the capers in olive oil and drain on paper towels. Arrange pepper diamonds on plates. Sprinkle with capers and drizzle each plate with 2 tbs of charcoal oil each. Arrange drained fish filets and serve.

Eismeerkabeljau auf Paprikakompott mit Holzkohleöl und Amalfi-Zitrone

Für 4 Personen

150 ml Pflanzenöl
50 g Holzkohle
5 rote Paprikaschoten
2 Schalotten
1 Knoblauchzehe
50 g Chorizo
3 EL Olivenöl
1 unbehandelte Zitrone
¼ TL geräuchertes Paprikapulver
¼ TL gemahlener Kreuzkümmel
1 Lorbeerblatt
Meersalz, Pfeffer
1 Msp Harissa
Saft von ½ eingelegten Amalfi-Zitrone
4 geschuppte Eismeer-Kabeljaufilets mit Haut (à 150 g)
1 EL Butter
1 Zweig Thymian
1 EL Kapern
Olivenöl zum Frittieren

Das Öl auf 60 °C erwärmen, die Holzkohle in kleinere Stücke zerteilen und mit dem erwärmten Öl übergießen. Zugedeckt ca. 24 Std. ziehen lassen und anschließend passieren.

Paprikaschoten waschen, mit einem Sparschäler häuten und putzen. Die Schalen und Abschnitte pürieren und anschließend durch ein feines Tuch passieren. Die Paprikaschoten in Rauten schneiden. Schalotten und Knoblauchzehe schälen. Zusammen mit der Chorizo in feine Würfel schneiden und in 1 EL Olivenöl anbraten. Paprikarauten zugeben und kurz mit anbraten. Paprikapulver, Kreuzkümmel, Lorbeerblatt sowie fein abgeriebene Zitronenschale zugeben und alles mit anrösten. Mit Salz, Pfeffer, Harissa und Zitronensaft würzen. Anschließend die Paprikarauten ca. 10 Min. bissfest garen. Paprikasaft zugeben, aufkochen, auf die gewünschte Konsistenz reduzieren und anschließend abschmecken.

Die Fischfilets waschen und trocken tupfen. Auf der Hautseite im restlichen Olivenöl langsam kross anbraten. Wenden, Butter und Thymianzweig in die Pfanne geben und bei mittlerer Hitze ca. 5 Min. garen. Anschließend mit Salz würzen.

Die Kapern in Olivenöl frittieren und auf Küchenpapier abtropfen lassen. Die Paprikarauten auf je einem Teller anrichten. Mit einigen Kapern bestreuen und mit jeweils 2 EL Holzkohleöl beträufeln. Die abgetropften Fischfilets darauf anrichten und servieren.

Crowned with a Michelin Star, this restaurant on the fifth floor of *The Mandala Hotel* offers culinary enjoyment in a casual atmosphere. The kitchen serves light Mediterranean and international meals and their wine list includes more than 400 items. Light floods through the *Facil* with its glass walls and skylight and fine materials such as natural-stone floors characterize its interior. The restaurant has room for 48 guests, with 20 more seats in the hotel garden accessible through sliding doors.

Mit einem Michelin-Stern gekrönt, bietet das Restaurant in der fünften Etage des *The Mandala Hotel* kulinarischen Genuss in ungezwungenem Rahmen. Die Küche serviert leichte mediterrane und internationale Speisen, die Weinkarte umfasst über 400 Positionen. Licht durchflutet das Restaurant *Facil* mit seinen Glaswänden und dem Oberlicht, sein Inneres ist durch edle Materialien wie Natursteinboden gekennzeichnet. 48 Gäste können hier empfangen werden, und weitere 20 im Hotelgarten, der durch Schiebetüren erreicht wird.

Salvatore Loi
Fasano
São Paulo, Brazil

Salvatore Loi was born in Sardinia, Italy. From an early age he was influenced by the exuberance of the gastronomic products his region offers, especially fish and seafood. After three years at Hotel School he moved to Milan where he launched his career in gastronomy. Since then he has worked in several distinguished restaurants—*Hotel Palace de Milano* (Milan), *Hotel Villa d'Este* (Como), *Hotel Meurice* (Paris), *Hotel Alfonso XIII* (Seville), and *Hotel Pitrizza* (Porto Cervo) among others—and with chefs such as Gualtiero Marchesi, Ângelo Paracucchi, Valentino Mercantilli, Cesare Chessorti (*Hotel Villa d'Este*) and Sergio Mei (*Hotel Four Seasons*, Milan). It was Sergio Mei who introduced Loi to Rogerio Fasano in 1999. Since then he has been the chef responsible for the *Fasano Restaurant*, however he also oversees the menus of all the other restaurants that belong to the *Fasano* Group. He has been awarded Chef of the Year five times by top publications in Brazil including Veja, Gula, and 4 Rodas guide.

Salvatore Loi wurde auf Sardinien geboren. Die Fülle an gastronomischen Produkten, die seine Region zu bieten hat, insbesondere Fisch und Meeresfrüchte, beeinflussten ihn bereits in jungem Alter. Nach drei Jahren auf der Hotelfachschule ging er nach Mailand – das war der Beginn seiner Karriere in der Gastronomie. Seitdem hat er in vielen angesehenen Restaurants gearbeitet – *Hotel Palace de Milano* (Mailand), *Hotel Villa d'Este* (Como), *Hotel Meurice* (Paris), *Hotel Alfonso XIII* (Sevilla) und *Hotel Pitrizza* (Porto Cervo), um nur einige zu nennen – und mit Köchen wie Gualtiero Marchesi, Ângelo Paracucchi, Valentino Mercantilli, Cesare Chessorti (*Hotel Villa d'Este*) und Sergio Mei (*Hotel Four Seasons*, Mailand) kooperiert. Letzterer stellte ihn 1999 Rogerio Fasano vor. Seither ist Loi verantwortlich für das *Fasano Restaurant*, überwacht aber auch die Menüauswahl aller anderen zur *Fasano*-Gruppe gehörenden Restaurants. Fünf Mal wurde er bereits von führenden Fachzeitschriften in Brasilien zum Chef of the Year ernannt, darunter Veja, Gula und 4 Rodas.

Spaghetti alla Chitarra con Ragu d'Agnello e Spugnole

Serves 4

4 oz morel mushrooms
4 sprigs of thyme
4 stems of parsley
5 tomatoes
8 lamb chops (approx. 1 ½ oz each)
salt, black pepper
4 oz butter
1 ¾ c lamb stock
1 lb 2 oz spaghetti
⅓ c 2 tbs olive oil

Clean mushrooms thoroughly, chop larger ones if necessary. Rinse thyme and parsley and shake off excess water, pluck off and mince the leaves. Blanch tomatoes in boiling water, rinse, peel, remove the seeds and dice.

Season lamb chops with salt and pepper. Heat the butter in a hot pan, sear the lamb chops one after the other for 2 min. each side until golden brown, then remove chops and keep warm. Add diced tomatoes, mushrooms and lamb stock and reduce stock to half.

Cook spaghetti in plenty of salted water until al dente and drain. Add pasta, thyme and parsley to the sauce. Smooth the sauce by adding olive oil and mix everything well.

Season again to taste and serve with two lamb chops each.

Spaghetti alla Chitarra con Ragu d'Agnello e Spugnole

Für 4 Personen

120 g Morcheln
4 Zweige Thymian
4 Stängel Petersilie
5 Tomaten
8 Lammkoteletts (à ca. 50 g)
Salz, schwarzer Pfeffer
120 g Butter
400 ml Lammfond
500 g Spaghetti
100 ml Olivenöl

Die Morcheln gut säubern, große eventuell klein schneiden. Thymian und Petersilie waschen, trocken schütteln, Blätter abzupfen und fein hacken. Die Tomaten mit kochendem Wasser überbrühen, abschrecken, häuten, entkernen und in feine Würfel schneiden.

Die einzelnen Lammkoteletts mit Salz und Pfeffer würzen. In einer heißen Pfanne anschließend portionsweise in Butter von beiden Seiten 2 Min. goldbraun anbraten, herausnehmen und warm halten. Die Tomatenwürfel mit den Morcheln sowie Lammfond in die Pfanne geben und den Fond zur Hälfte reduzieren.

Spaghetti in reichlich Salzwasser bissfest garen und abtropfen lassen. Unter die Sauce mischen, dann Thymian und Petersilie zugeben. Mit Olivenöl verfeinern und alles gut mischen.

Nochmals abschmecken und zusammen mit jeweils 2 Lammkoteletts servieren.

This restaurant on the ground floor of the luxury hotel of the same name has won the highest number of awards in the city. It is said to offer the best Italian cuisine in South America and its variety is praised for its typical dishes from all regions. In addition to the traditional meals, the *Fasano* also serves contemporary creations. Diners can choose among five menus. The restaurant with its 80 seats also stands out because of its classic elegant yet discreet ambience. The bar hosts live music every night.

Das Restaurant im Erdgeschoss des gleichnamigen Luxushotels ist das mit den meisten Auszeichnungen der Stadt. Es soll die beste italienische Küche Südamerikas bieten, deren Vielfalt durch typische Speisen aus allen Regionen zelebriert wird. Neben traditionellen Gerichten werden auch zeitgenössische Kreationen serviert. Fünf Menüs stehen dabei zur Auswahl. Das Lokal mit seinen 80 Sitzplätzen besticht durch sein klassisch elegantes gleichwohl schlichtes Ambiente. An der Bar wird jede Nacht Live-Musik geboten.

Andrew Parkinson
Fifteen
London, UK

Andrew Parkinson is the Executive Head Chef of *Fifteen* London where he oversees two restaurants: the Trattoria and the Dining Room. With 22 years of cooking experience under his belt, he plays a major role in the future of *Fifteen* restaurants worldwide. Parkinson came to *Fifteen* with a wealth of experience and knowledge as author of "Cutting it Fine", a book describing his rise through the ranks and the running of a professional kitchen. Not only does he manage a team of 25 professional chefs, but also mentors a team of 15 apprentices every 18 months as part of a pioneering apprenticeship scheme for young people. His style of food is best described as Italian modern classic. He has a passion for researching food culture, particularly its historic origins, hence he manages to source only the best premium ingredients for *Fifteen's* customers. Prior to joining *Fifteen* Parkinson worked as Head Chef at restaurants such as *Bertorelli's*, *Soho Soho*, *Quaglino's* and *Odettes*.

In seiner Funktion als Executive Head Chef im *Fifteen* London ist Andrew Parkinson für zwei Restaurants zuständig: Trattoria und Dining Room. Mit 22 Jahren Berufserfahrung spielt er eine wichtige Rolle in der Zukunft der *Fifteen*-Restaurants weltweit. Als Parkinson zu *Fifteen* kam, verfügte er bereits über einen reichen Erfahrungsschatz und viel Wissen – auch als Autor des Buchs „Cutting it Fine", das seinen beruflichen Werdegang und den Alltag in einer professionellen Küche beschreibt. Er leitet nicht nur ein Team von 25 Profiköchen, sondern betreut auch noch alle 18 Monate eine Gruppe von 15 Auszubildenden als Teil eines innovativen Ausbildungsmodells für junge Leute. Was das Essen betrifft, lässt sich sein Stil am besten als klassisch Italienisch mit modernem Touch beschreiben. Zu seinen Leidenschaften gehört das Erforschen von Esskulturen, vor allem deren historische Ursprünge. Ihm gelingt es daher, nur die besten und hochwertigsten Zutaten für die Gäste der *Fifteen*-Restaurants auszuwählen. Vor seiner Zeit bei *Fifteen* arbeitete Parkinson als Küchenchef in Restaurants wie dem *Bertorelli's*, *Soho Soho*, *Quaglino's* und *Odettes*.

Christmas Salad

Serves 4

1 bunch of watercress
1 bunch of dandelion or rocket leaves
12 Radicchio di Treviso leaves
4 mandarin oranges
6 tbs olive oil
2 tbs balsamic vinegar
salt, pepper
12 slices of bacon
1 oz Parmesan

Clean, wash and spin watercress, dandelion or rocket and radicchio leaves. If necessary, cut larger leaves into smaller pieces and place everything in a bowl.

Peel mandarin oranges and remove the white skin, cut into thin slices and mix with the other leaves.

Add olive oil and balsamic vinegar and mix. Season with salt and pepper. Arrange salad on four plates and place three slices of bacon between the leaves.

Grate some Parmesan on top and serve.

Weihnachtssalat

Für 4 Personen

1 Bund Brunnenkresse
1 Bund Löwenzahn oder Rucola
12 Treviso-Salatblätter
4 Klementinen
6 EL Olivenöl
2 EL Balsamico-Essig
Salz, Pfeffer
12 Scheiben Schinkenspeck
30 g Parmesan

Brunnenkresse, Löwenzahn oder Rucola sowie Treviso-Salatblätter putzen, waschen und trocken schleudern. Falls nötig, größere Blätter zerkleinern und alles zusammen in eine Schüssel geben.

Die Klementinen samt der weißen Haut schälen, in dünne Scheiben schneiden und mit den Salatblättern vermengen.

Mit Olivenöl und Balsamico-Essig mischen und mit Salz und Pfeffer würzen. Den Salat auf vier Teller verteilen und jeweils drei Scheiben Schinkenspeck zwischen den Salatblättern anrichten.

Etwas Parmesan über alles hobeln und servieren.

Founded by Jamie Oliver and opened in 2002 as a project with young people, the restaurant now has three international branches. It offers modern Italian cuisine and is divided on two levels into a dining room and a trattoria. The retro-style design of the dining room with its graffiti elements and open kitchen creates an easy-going atmosphere. The menus vary daily and a special sample menu is offered in the evenings. The trattoria on the ground level also serves breakfast. All profits from the restaurant go to a registered charity.

Das von Jamie Oliver gegründete und 2002 als Projekt mit Jugendlichen eröffnete Restaurant, bietet moderne italienische Küche und hat inzwischen drei internationale Ableger. Es ist auf zwei Ebenen in einen Speisesaal und eine Trattoria unterteilt. Das Design des Speisesaals im Retro-Stil schafft mit seinen Graffiti-Elementen und der offenen Küche eine legere Atmosphäre. Die Menüs wechseln täglich, abends gibt es ein spezielles Probiermenü. In der Trattoria im Erdgeschoss wird auch Frühstück serviert. Alle Gewinne des Restaurants werden an einen eingetragenen Wohlfahrtsverband gespendet.

Christopher Lee
Gilt

New York, USA

Christopher Lee garnered national attention as the Executive Chef at *The Striped Bass* in Philadelphia. He received the James Beard "2005 Rising Star Chef of the Year" award and was named one of Food & Wine Magazine's "Best New Chefs for 2006". That year, the Long Island native returned to his New York roots to take the helm as Executive Chef at *Gilt* Restaurant in the *New York Palace Hotel*. A graduate of San Francisco's California Culinary Academy in 2000, he shined as a Chef de Cuisine under Cornelius Gallagher at *Oceana*, until he was hand-selected to be Chef de Cuisine at *The Striped Bass*. There he rose to the position of Executive Chef, drawing on his prior experience at *Jean Georges*, *Daniel*, and San Francisco's *Fifth Floor*. He is interested in bringing out the best flavors in food by using farm-fresh products and creating plates that are works of art. He uses everyday ingredients in a New Millennium way, infusing excitement into classic dishes.

Als Executive Chef des Restaurants *The Striped Bass* in Philadelphia erlangte Christopher Lee nationale Aufmerksamkeit. Er erhielt von der James-Beard-Stiftung die Auszeichnung „2005 Rising Star Chef of the Year" und die Zeitschrift Food & Wine listete ihn unter den „Best New Chefs for 2006". Im gleichen Jahr kehrte der von Long Island stammende Lee nach New York zu seinen Wurzeln zurück und übernahm im *Gilt* Restaurant im *New York Palace Hotel* als Executive Chef das Kommando. 2000 machte er seinen Abschluss an der California Culinary Academy in San Francisco, glänzte danach als Küchenchef unter Cornelius Gallagher im *Oceana* und wurde schließlich zum Küchenchef des *The Striped Bass* auserwählt. Dort stieg er in die Position des Executive Chefs auf und konnte auf seine im *Jean Georges*, *Daniel* und *Fifth Floor* in San Francisco gesammelten Erfahrungen zurückgreifen. Es liegt ihm am Herzen, den bestmöglichen Geschmack aus den Nahrungsmitteln zu holen. Dafür verwendet er frische Erzeugnisse und kreiert seine Gerichte als wahre Kunstwerke. Er verwendet alltägliche Zutaten, aber auf eine vollkommen neue Weise, sodass er ein spannendes Element in klassische Gerichte zaubert.

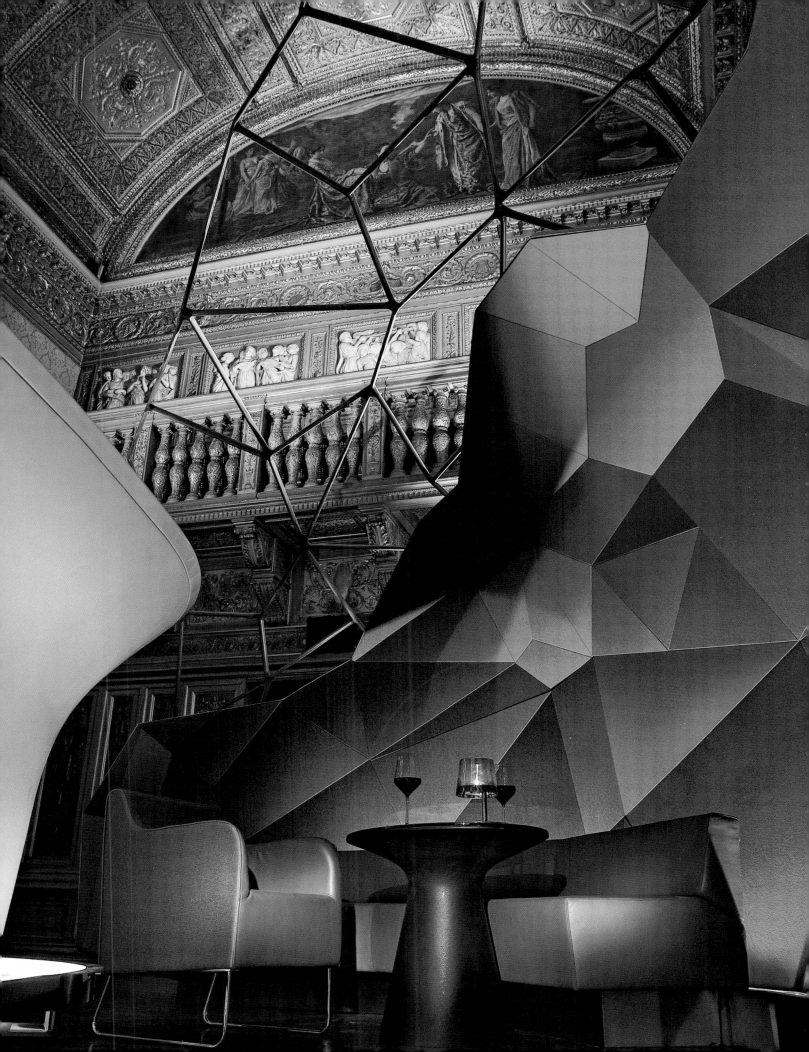

Yellowfin Tuna "Wellington" with Wild Mushrooms, Flat Leaf Spinach and Red Wine Sauce

Serves 4

4 sheets of frozen pastry (4 oz each)
1 lb 2 oz mixed wild mushrooms
4 shallots
4 tbs oil
1 c white wine
salt, pepper
4 yellowfin tuna filets (3.3 oz each)
40 large, flat spinach leaves
flour for preparation
2 egg whites for glazing
2 ½ c red wine
½ c 2 tbs port
2 oz ice-cold butter

Defrost pastry sheets. Clean mushrooms and slice thinly. Peel and dice shallots. Sear mushrooms in oil until any excess liquid from the mushrooms has been boiled down. Add shallots and sear briefly together with the mushrooms. Add white wine and leave to reduce. Season with salt and pepper. Remove mushrooms and set aside to cool.

Clean spinach and blanch in plenty of salted water for approx. 10 seconds, rinse in ice-cold water and squeeze gently.

Place 4 pieces of plastic wrap (8 x 12 in. each) on the kitchen worktop. Arrange the spinach leaves into rectangles of 6 x 8 in. size, allowing the edges to overlap slightly. Pat dry with paper towels. Spread a layer of mushrooms on each rectangle, leaving approx. 1 ¼ in. around the edge.

Season tuna filets with salt and pepper and place at the one end of each rectangle. Use the plastic wrap to roll the tuna with the spinach and the mushrooms and gently press edges together. Place in the fridge for about 10 min.

Roll out the individual pastry sheets on a floured surface into 6 x 6 in. rectangles and round the edges slightly. Remove the plastic wrap from the tuna rolls. Place on pastry and roll until completely covered with dough. Fold edges over.

Line a baking tray with parchment paper and place rolls onto the tray. Glaze with egg white and bake in a preheated convection oven at 430 °F. Bake until cooked as preferred: for a raw filling, bake for 12 min., for medium 14 min., for almost done 16 min. and for well done 18 min.

For the sauce: bring red wine and port to a boil and reduce to ¼ c. Whisk in butter in small amounts and season with salt and pepper.

Yellow Fin-Thunfisch „Wellington" mit Waldpilzen, Blattspinat und Rotweinsauce

Für 4 Personen

4 tiefgefrorene Blätterteigscheiben (à 120 g)
500 g gemischte Waldpilze
4 Schalotten
4 EL Öl
250 ml Weißwein
Salz, Pfeffer
4 Yellow Fin-Thunfisch-Filets (à 100 g)
40 große flache Spinatblätter
Mehl zum Bearbeiten
2 Eiweiß zum Bestreichen
600 ml Rotwein
150 ml Portwein
60 g eiskalte Butter

Die Blätterteigscheiben auftauen lassen. Pilze putzen und in dünne Scheiben schneiden. Die Schalotten schälen und fein würfeln. Die Pilze in Öl anbraten, bis das ausgetretene Wasser verdampft ist. Dann die Schalotten zugeben und kurz mitbraten. Mit Weißwein ablöschen und fast vollständig verdampfen lassen. Mit Salz und Pfeffer würzen. Anschließend die Pilze herausnehmen und abkühlen lassen.

Den geputzten Spinat in reichlich Salzwasser ca. 10 Sek. blanchieren, in Eiswasser abschrecken und leicht ausdrücken.

Jeweils 4 Stücke Frischhaltefolie (à 20 x 30 cm) auf der Arbeitsplatte auslegen. Die Spinatblätter leicht überlappend nebeneinander legen, sodass vier 15 x 20 cm große Rechtecke entstehen. Mit Küchenpapier trocken tupfen. Dann jeweils eine Schicht Pilze darüber verteilen und dabei rundherum etwa einen 3 cm breiten Rand freilassen.

Die Thunfisch-Filets mit Salz und Pfeffer würzen und jeweils an ein Ende der Rechtecke legen. Mit Hilfe der Frischhaltefolie den Thunfisch langsam zusammen mit dem Spinat und den Pilzen einrollen und die Enden fest andrücken. Anschließend ca. 10 Min. kalt stellen.

Die Blätterteigscheiben einzeln auf einer bemehlten Arbeitsfläche etwas dünner zu etwa 15 x 15 cm großen Rechtecken ausrollen und die Enden etwas abrunden. Die Thunfischrollen ohne Folie auf die Blätterteigstücke geben und einrollen, bis sie ganz mit Teig bedeckt sind und die Enden zusammenklappen.

Auf ein mit Backpapier ausgelegtes Backblech geben, mit Eiweiß bestreichen und im vorgeheizten Backofen bei 220 °C Heißluft backen. Je nach gewünschtem Gargrad für einen rohen Kern 12 Min., für medium 14 Min., für fast durchgebraten 16 Min. und für durchgebraten 18 Min. garen.

Für die Sauce Rotwein und Portwein aufkochen und auf 60 ml reduzieren. Butter portionsweise unterrühren und mit Salz und Pfeffer abschmecken.

This fine restaurant in the historic building of the *New York Palace Hotel* offers new American cuisine with focus on the seasons. Classic elements are combined with modern ones. You can choose between three-, five- or seven-course menus. One of *Gilt's* specialties – in addition to its wide selection of wines – is its range of rare brands of teas. The intimate restaurant has space for 52 guests. The futuristic design of its bar and lounge forms an exciting contrast to its splendid Neo-Renaissance interior.

Das edle Restaurant im historischen Gebäude des *New York Palace Hotel* bietet neue amerikanische Küche mit saisonalen Schwerpunkten. Klassisches wird mit modernen Elementen kombiniert, man kann zwischen Drei-, Fünf- oder Sieben-Gang-Menüs wählen. Eine Besonderheit: Neben der breiten Weinauswahl werden auch seltene Teesorten angeboten. 52 Gäste haben in dem intimen Restaurant Platz. Die futuristische Raumskulptur der Bar und Lounge bildet einen aufregenden Kontrast zu dem prachtvollen Neo-Renaissance-Interieur.

Siegfried Kröpfl
Restaurant Imperial
Vienna, Austria

Siegfried Kröpfl was born in the Tyrol and served his apprenticeship in Vorarlberg. By 1977 he had discovered a great teacher in Werner Matt at the Vienna *Hilton* where he worked for five years. After a year of seasonal challenges in Carinthia, Styria and Tyrol, he returned to the *Hilton* to head up banqueting and the *Prinz Eugen* restaurant. From 1983 to 1985 he delighted many celebrities, including Queen Elizabeth, with his exquisite culinary delights at the *Harbour Castle* hotel, Toronto. Returning to Austria he became Sous Chef at the Vienna *Hilton*, later assisting Eduard Mitsche, then in 1993 he was made Chef de Cuisine. At the *Hotel Imperial*, Kröpfl's culinary skills range from hearty fare to the exotically elaborate. With a 30-strong team he oversees the culinary management of the multi award-winning *Restaurant Imperial* as well as banqueting, catering and the traditional *Café Imperial*.

Siegfried Kröpfl wurde in Tirol geboren und absolvierte seine Ausbildung in Vorarlberg. Im Wiener *Hilton Hotel*, wo er insgesamt fünf Jahre arbeitete, hatte er 1977 in Werner Matt seinen großen Lehrmeister gefunden. Nach einem Jahr Saisonanstellungen in Kärnten, der Steiermark und Tirol kehrte Kröpfl ins *Hilton* zurück und übernahm die Leitung für Bankettveranstaltungen und für das Restaurant *Prinz Eugen*. Von 1983 bis 1985 war er im *Harbour Castle* in Toronto tätig, wo er viele berühmte Persönlichkeiten, darunter Queen Elizabeth, mit seinen exquisiten kulinarischen Köstlichkeiten begeisterte. Nach seiner Rückkehr nach Österreich übernahm Kröpfl die Position des Sous Chefs im Wiener *Hilton Hotel*, wurde später die rechte Hand Eduard Mitsches und 1993 schließlich Küchenchef. Im *Hotel Imperial* reicht Kröpfls kulinarische Bandbreite von herzhaften Speisen bis zu exotischen Raffinessen. Mit einem Team von 30 Mitarbeitern hat er die kulinarische Leitung im mehrfach ausgezeichneten *Restaurant Imperial* inne und ist außerdem für Bankette, Catering und das traditionsreiche *Café Imperial* verantwortlich.

Blueberry Pancake with Marinated Berries

Serves 1

For the pancake
3.3 oz fresh blueberries
3 eggs
salt
1 vanilla bean
1 lemon, untreated
2 ½ oz curd cheese
½ c milk
¼ c cream
¾ oz sugar
2.3 oz flour
1.3 oz butter
1.3 oz powdered sugar

For the marinated berries
3.3 oz fresh mixed berries, e.g. raspberries, blackberries
1 tsp powdered sugar
1 tsp lemon juice
1 tsp orange liqueur

Sort and wash the blueberries. Separate the eggs and beat the egg white with a pinch of salt until stiff. Split the vanilla bean lengthwise and scrape out the seeds.

Rinse the lemon under hot water and grate some lemon zest. Mix curd cheese, egg yolks, milk and cream and stir thoroughly. Add sugar, a pinch of salt, vanilla seeds and lemon zest. Add flour and stir. Carefully fold in the stiff egg white. Melt butter in a pan, add the mixture and garnish with blueberries.

Bake in a preheated convection oven at 355 °F for approx. 10 min. until golden brown. In the meantime, sort and wash the berries.

Mix with powdered sugar, lemon juice and orange liqueur and set aside to steep. When cooking time is up, remove pancake from the oven, cut into pieces, sprinkle with powdered sugar and serve with the marinated berries.

Heidelbeerschmarrn mit marinierten Beeren

Für 1 Portion

Schmarrn
100 g frische Heidelbeeren
3 Eier
Salz
1 Vanilleschote
1 unbehandelte Zitrone
80 g Quark
125 ml Milch
60 ml Sahne
20 g Zucker
70 g Mehl
40 g Butter
40 g Puderzucker

Marinierte Beeren
100 g frische gemischte Beeren, z. B. Himbeeren, Brombeeren
1 TL Puderzucker
1 TL Zitronensaft
1 TL Orangenlikör

Die Heidelbeeren verlesen und waschen. Eier trennen und das Eiweiß mit 1 Prise Salz steif schlagen. Vanilleschote halbieren und das Mark herauskratzen.

Die Zitrone heiß abwaschen und etwas Schale abreiben. Quark mit Eigelb, Milch und Sahne gut verrühren. Zucker, 1 Prise Salz, Vanillemark und Zitronenschale zugeben. Mehl unterrühren und das geschlagene Eiweiß vorsichtig unterheben. In einer Pfanne die Butter zerlassen, den Teig zugeben und mit Heidelbeeren belegen.

Im vorgeheizten Backofen bei 180 °C Heißluft ca. 10 Min. goldbraun backen. In der Zwischenzeit die Beeren verlesen und waschen.

Mit Puderzucker, Zitronensaft und Orangenlikör mischen und ziehen lassen. Nach Ende der Garzeit den Schmarrn herausnehmen, zerteilen, mit Puderzucker bestäuben und zusammen mit den marinierten Beeren servieren.

Impeccable service and cuisine at its finest—you would hardly expect anything less from the *Restaurant Imperial*. After all, this wonderfully traditional fine dining restaurant belongs to the *Hotel Imperial* which was built as the private residence of the Prince of Württemberg in 1863. The finest culinary delicacies are sure to entice the palates of the restaurant's distinguished guests while they enjoy the elegant atmosphere. Classic Viennese cuisine is creatively paired with exotic culinary art and the wine list holds many a surprise in store for the visitors; take the excellent sweet wines that complement exquisite desserts, for instance. The stylish and exclusive ambiance extends to the *Café Imperial* and the *Bar Maria Theresia*, the heart of the establishment, in particular. Guests experience truly Imperial moments among regulars as well as eminent personalities from the world of politics, business, culture and entertainment. Different function rooms including the Marble Hall and the majestic Festival Hall are available for events. First class service flavored with sweet Viennese charm.

Service und Gastronomie vom Feinsten – etwas anderes würde man im *Restaurant Imperial* kaum erwarten, schließlich gehört das traditionsreiche, gediegene Lokal zum *Hotel Imperial*, das 1863 als Privatresidenz des Prinzen von Württemberg erbaut wurde. In erlesener Atmosphäre werden die Gaumen der illustren Gäste mit kulinarischer Raffinesse verwöhnt. Die traditionelle Wiener Küche geht eine kreative Liaison mit exotischer Kochkunst ein und die Weinkarte hält so manche Entdeckung bereit, beispielsweise hervorragende Süßweine zu ausgesuchten Desserts. Die elegante Atmosphäre setzt sich im *Café Imperial* und vor allem auch in der *Bar Maria Theresia*, dem Herzstück des Hauses, fort. Besucher erleben hier unter Staatsgästen, bekannten Persönlichkeiten aus Wirtschaft und Kultur sowie den Stammgästen wahrhaft imperiale Momente. Für Veranstaltungen stehen verschiedene Salons, wie der Marmorsaal oder der aristokratische Hallensalon, zur Verfügung. Erstklassige Servicequalität gewürzt mit der Süße des Wiener Charmes.

Gianni Caprioli
Isola bar & grill
Hong Kong, China

Giandomenico (Gianni) Caprioli, one of Italy's renowned Family Chefs, heads the kitchen at Gaia Group's *Isola bar & grill*. Born into a family of cooks in Potenza, Caprioli trained at a Hotel School and began his career in his brother's restaurant. He developed his skills in homemade pastas and Romagna-style cooking in San Marino in 1988, however his cooking truly blossomed while working under Master Chef Gino Angelini at the *Grand Hotel des Bains* in Riccione from 1992 to 1994. His reputation earned him a consultancy to the Rex Group of restaurants in the USA, managing and training staff. In 1997 he returned to Riccione as chef at *Ristorante Azzurra*, working with the revered and innovative chef Gianfranco Vissani. In 2000 he left for Los Angeles for the launch of *Osteria Angelini*. Here his skills came to the attention of the Agnelli family (owners of Fiat) who hired him as their personal chef.

Giandomenico (Gianni) Caprioli, einer der angesehensten Family Chefs Italiens, zeichnet für die Leitung der Küche des Isola bar & grill der Gaia-Gruppe verantwortlich. In Potenza in eine Familie von Köchen hineingeboren, besuchte Caprioli die Hotelfachschule und startete seine berufliche Laufbahn im Restaurant seines Bruders. Während seines Aufenthalts in San Marino im Jahr 1988 entwickelte er seine Fähigkeiten im Zubereiten hausgemachter Pasta und der von der Romagna beeinflussten Küche. Seine Kochkünste gelangten jedoch erst unter Meisterkoch Gino Angelini zu voller Blüte – im *Grand Hotel des Bains* in Riccione von 1992 bis 1994. Sein guter Ruf brachte ihm eine Beraterstelle bei der Rex-Restaurantgruppe in den USA ein, wo er Mitarbeiter schulte und betreute. 1997 kehrte er nach Riccione zurück und wurde Koch im *Ristorante Azzurra*, wo er mit dem namhaften und innovativen Koch Gianfranco Vissani zusammenarbeitete. 2000 kehrte er Riccione den Rücken und ging nach Los Angeles zur Eröffnung der *Osteria Angelini*. Dort wurde die Familie Agnelli, Besitzer des Fiat-Konzerns, auf seine kulinarischen Fähigkeiten aufmerksam und stellte ihn als ihren persönlichen Koch ein.

Rigatoni with Lobster

Serves 4

1lb 2 oz rigatoni
salt
2 lobster tails (approx. 5 oz each)
1 shallot
2 cloves of garlic
2 tbs olive oil
4 tbs white wine
10 oz cherry tomatoes
pepper
basil to garnish

Cook the pasta as directed on the package in a large pot of salted water until al dente, rinse and drain.

Cut the lobster tails into bite-sized pieces. Peel the shallot and the garlic, dice them and sweat them in olive oil. Add the lobster pieces, pour in the white wine and bring to a boil.

Leave to cook under a medium heat until the liquid has almost completely evaporated. Wash the cherry tomatoes, cut them into four, add them to the pot and season to taste. Mix the rigatoni with the lobster sauce, heat and, again, season to taste.

Serve on large pasta dishes with basil garnish.

Rigatoni mit Hummer

Für 4 Personen

500 g Rigatoni
Salz
2 Hummerschwänze (à ca. 150 g)
1 Schalotte
2 Knoblauchzehen
2 EL Olivenöl
4 EL Weißwein
280 g Kirschtomaten
Pfeffer
Basilikumblätter zum Dekorieren

Die Pasta in reichlich Salzwasser nach Packungsanweisung bissfest garen, abschrecken und abtropfen lassen.

Hummerschwänze in mundgerechte Stücke schneiden. Schalotte und Knoblauchzehen schälen, in feine Würfel schneiden und in Olivenöl anschwitzen. Die Hummerstücke zugeben, mit Weißwein aufgießen und aufkochen.

Bei mittlerer Hitze weiterkochen, bis die Flüssigkeit fast vollständig verdampft ist. Kirschtomaten waschen, vierteln, zugeben und würzen. Die Rigatoni unter die Hummersauce heben, heiß werden lassen und nochmals abschmecken.

Auf großen Pastatellern anrichten und mit Basilikumblättern garniert servieren.

Opened in 2004, this restaurant at the harbor impresses with a wonderful view of the city skyline through windows extending from floor to ceiling. Add to that a large outside terrace. The interior is elegant and kept in white. Filigree wall and ceiling panels made of white metal immediately catch the eye. The kitchen offers Italian dishes like pizzas, pastas and barbeque dishes, which are simple and rustic, showcasing freshest best quality produce—or as the Head Chef Gianni Caprioli puts it, "common ingredients cooked uncommonly well." Open, marble-top cooking stations allow you to watch the cooks perform their work.

2004 eröffnet, beeindruckt das am Hafen gelegene Restaurant mit einem herrlichen Ausblick auf die Skyline der Stadt, durch Fenster, die vom Boden bis zur Decke reichen. Zudem gibt es eine große Außenterrasse. Das Interieur ist elegant und in Weiß gehalten. Blickfang ist eine filigrane Wand- und Deckenverkleidung aus weißem Metall. Die Küche bietet italienische Speisen wie Pizza, Pasta und Grillgerichte, die einfach und rustikal sind und für die die frischesten und besten Qualitätsprodukte verwendet werden – oder, um es mit den Worten des Küchenchefs Gianni Caprioli zu sagen: „Gewöhnliche Zutaten ungewöhnlich gut zubereitet." Durch offene, marmorverkleidete Kochstationen sieht man den Köchen bei der Arbeit zu.

Gene Kato
Japonais
Chicago, USA

Gene Kato, Executive Chef/Partner of *Japonais* was born and raised in North Carolina. He was inspired to cook at an early stage by his Japanese parents who reinforced the importance of family meals, Japanese customs and their traditional cuisine. Kato brings a progressive, yet fundamentally classic culinary approach to *Japonais* with dishes that "pay homage to my Japanese heritage but also push the envelope with unique flavor pairings." After earning an Associate's Degree in Culinary Arts at Central Piedmont Community College in Charlotte, Kato spent a year in Japan continuing his education. Once back in the United States, he worked as Chef de Cuisine at *Mimosa Grill* (Charlotte, North Carolina) and also at *Upstream* (Charleston, South Carolina). While in the Carolinas, Kato was exposed to both French and Southern cuisine, yet he always remained mindful of his Japanese roots. Eventually he moved to Chicago where he and his business partner Miae Lim opened *Ohba*, which was shortly followed by the opening of *Japonais* and *The Mirage* in Las Vegas.

Gene Kato, Executive Chef und Partner im Japonais wuchs in North Carolina auf. Seine Eltern legten viel Wert auf Familienessen, japanische Bräuche und die traditionelle Küche ihres Heimatlandes und weckten in ihm schon früh den Wunsch, sich dem Kochen zu widmen. Kato bringt mit Gerichten „die meiner japanischen Herkunft huldigen, aber auch mit einzigartigen Geschmacksverbindungen Neues schaffen" einen progressiven, im Grunde dennoch klassischen kulinarischen Ansatz ins *Japonais*. Nach seinem Abschluss im Fachbereich Culinary Arts am Central Piedmont Community College in Charlotte setzte Kato seine Ausbildung ein Jahr lang in Japan fort. Zurück in den USA arbeitete Kato als Küchenchef im *Mimosa Grill* in Charlotte (North Carolina) und im *Upstream* in Charleston (South Carolina). Während dieser Zeit in North und South Carolina machte Kato sich sowohl mit der französischen Küche als auch mit der Südstaatenküche vertraut, blieb dabei jedoch stets seinen japanischen Wurzeln treu. Schließlich zog es ihn nach Chicago, wo er zusammen mit seinem Geschäftspartner Miae Lim das Restaurant *Ohba* eröffnete. Kurze Zeit später folgten das *Japonais* und das *The Mirage* in Las Vegas.

Chilean Sea Bass al Cartoccio

Serves 4

13.3 oz skinned sea bass filet
4 large button mushrooms (1 oz each)
4 spring onions
4 tbs butter (cold)
2 oz pickled bamboo shoots
2 cloves of garlic
4 tbs sake
8 tbs soy sauce
2 tsp aonori
black pepper

Wash the sea bass filets, dab them dry and cut them into bite-sized pieces. Clean the mushrooms. Clean the spring onions and cut into 1 in. pieces. Cut the butter into pieces. Fill four roasting bags with the ingredients and evenly spread the bamboo shoots on top.

To make the sauce, peel the cloves of garlic and finely dice them. Mix all the ingrdients thoroughly and season to taste. Add the sauce evenly to each roasting bag, then seal each bag tightly and pierce a small hole in the top of each bag. Cook in a preheated convection oven for 15 min. at approx. 300 °F.

Open the bags and serve the contents on plates.

Chilenischer Seebarsch al Cartoccio

Für 4 Personen

400 g gehäutetes Seebarschfilet
4 große Champignons (à 30 g)
4 Frühlingszwiebeln
4 EL kalte Butter
60 g eingelegte Bambussprossen
2 Knoblauchzehen
4 EL Sake
8 EL Sojasauce
2 TL Aonori
schwarzer Pfeffer

Die Seebarschfilets waschen, trocken tupfen und in mundgerechte Stücke schneiden. Champignons säubern. Die Frühlingszwiebeln putzen und in 2,5 cm lange Stücke schneiden. Butter in Stücke schneiden. 4 Bratbeutel jeweils mit den vorbereiteten Zutaten füllen und die Bambussprossen darüber verteilen.

Für die Sauce die Knoblauchzehen schälen und fein würfeln. Alle Zutaten gründlich miteinander vermischen und würzen. Die Sauce ebenfalls in die Bratbeutel verteilen, diese gut verschließen und in die Oberseite ein kleines Loch hineinstechen. Im vorgeheizten Backofen bei 150 °C Heißluft ca. 15 Min. garen.

Die Beutel öffnen und den Inhalt auf Tellern zum Servieren anrichten.

Located on the Chicago River, this restaurant offers both modern, progressive Japanese cuisine and sushi. It has received numerous awards, with Chicago Magazine crowning it "Best Restaurant" in 2005. Elegant materials like mahogany, leather and velvet create its elegant atmosphere. Japanese and European influences characterize its purist design. Its rooms are all about atmosphere: purity and serenity are two overarching themes in both the restaurant, and each of the two dining rooms, the "Red Dining Room" and the "Green Dining Room." There is a second *Japonais* in New York City.

Das am Chicago River gelegene Lokal bietet sowohl zeitgenössische japanische Küche als auch Sushi. Es hat diverse Auszeichnungen erhalten – vom Chicago Magazine wurde es 2005 zum besten Restaurant gekürt. Das intime Ambiente wird von eleganten Materialien wie Mahagoni, Leder und Samt bestimmt. Das puristische Design ist von japanischen und europäischen Einflüssen geprägt. Die Räume sind stimmungsvoll inszeniert: So gibt es einen „Red Dining Room" und einen „Green Dining Room". Das *Japonais* hat nun auch eine Niederlassung in New York.

Volker Eisenmann
Käfer-Schänke
Munich, Germany

Volker Eisenmann has been successfully calling the tune at the sophisticated *Käfer-Schänke* for five years. He has demonstrated his abilities in many different establishments during his professional career, from the officers' mess at the German Infantry School, a hotel and hotel school, right up to working as a Personal Chef for an automotive company. Greatly influenced by classic French cuisine which he discovered and learned to love for its variety and refinement at, among others, the Restaurant *Schweizer Stuben,* where he trained under Fritz Schilling, the 33-year old Head Chef is an advocate of traditional down-to-earth food. He focuses on the product itself using nothing but the best, genuine ingredients. He naturally explores modern cooking techniques without simply pursuing the latest craze. This philosophy has been successful with the highly demanding clientele at *Käfer-Schänke* for years.

Bereits seit fünf Jahren gibt Volker Eisenmann erfolgreich den guten Ton in der stilvollen *Käfer-Schänke* an. Während seiner bisherigen beruflichen Laufbahn hat er in den verschiedensten Betrieben sein Können unter Beweis gestellt, vom Offizierscasino der Schule der deutschen Infanterie über Hotel und Hotelfachschule bis hin zu Einsätzen als Privatkoch bei einem Automobilkonzern. Geprägt von der klassischen französischen Küche, die er unter anderem in dem Restaurant *Schweizer Stuben* bei Fritz Schilling in all ihrer Kunst und Vielfalt kennen- und schätzen lernte, ist der 33-jährige Küchenchef ein Verfechter einer bodenständigen, soliden Küche. Das Produkt als solches steht im Mittelpunkt und die besten Zutaten werden unverfälscht verarbeitet. Neueste Garmethoden werden selbstverständlich eingesetzt, jedoch nicht jeder Mode nachgeeifert. Eine Philosophie, die seit Jahren die anspruchsvolle Klientel der *Käfer-Schänke* überzeugt.

Red Mullet with Spiced Pancetta

Serves 4

Pot-au-feu
4 artichokes
a pinch of ascorbic acid
½ celery stalk
1 carrot
½ fennel bulb
4 shallots
2 cloves of garlic
3.3 oz Pancetta (Italian bacon)
5 tbs olive oil
1 c chicken stock
2 tbs white wine
2 tbs vermouth
10 cilantro seeds
juice of 1 lemon
1 bay leaf
milled black pepper
3.3 oz Taggia olives

Red Mullet
4 scaled, filleted red mullets (8–10 oz each)
salt, milled black pepper
juice of half a lemon
3 tbs olive oil
10 cloves of young garlic
1 sprig of thyme
1 sprig of rosemary

Clean the artichokes, remove the stem and leaves and pluck the straw-like hair of the flower. Add 4 cups of cold water and the ascorbic acid so that the artichoke bottoms are lightly covered. Clean the vegetables and finely dice them. Peel the shallots and the cloves of garlic and finely dice them.

Leave the artichoke bottoms to dry, finely cut them and lightly fry them with the Pancetta in 3 tbs of olive oil. Add the vegetables and garlic, add the chicken stock, white wine and vermouth and boil down to half the quantity. Add the cilantro, lemon juice and bay leaf.

Season with pepper and leave to simmer for approx. 20 min. Then, season with the remaining olive oil and add the olives. Wash and dab dry the red mullet and season inside and outside with salt and pepper and sprinkle with lemon juice. Peel the garlic. Sear the fish in a pan with olive oil, and add the cloves of garlic and herbs. Weight down the fish (e. g. with a pot) and fry on each side for 3–4 min.

Arrange the vegetables on a plate, place the fish on top of the vegetables and the Pancetta on top of the fish.

Serving suggestion: Home-made gnocchi with thyme.

Felsenrotbarbe mit gewürzter Pancetta

Für 4 Personen

Pot-au-feu
4 Artischocken
eine Prise Ascorbinsäure (1 g)
½ Stange Staudensellerie
1 Karotte
½ Fenchelknolle
4 Schalotten
2 Knoblauchzehen
100 g Pancetta (italienischer Bauchspeck)
5 EL Olivenöl
250 ml Hühnerbrühe
30 ml Weißwein
30 ml Wermut
10 Koriandersamen
Saft von 1 Zitrone
1 Lorbeerblatt
schwarzer Pfeffer aus der Mühle
100 g Taggiasche-Oliven

Felsenrotbarbe
4 geschuppte, hohl ausgelöste Felsenrotbarben (à 250 – 300 g)
Salz, schwarzer Pfeffer aus der Mühle
Saft von ½ Zitrone
3 EL Olivenöl
10 junge Knoblauchzehen
1 Zweig Thymian
1 Zweig Rosmarin

Die Artischocken putzen, Stiele, äußere Blätter entfernen und die strohigen Blütenfäden herauszupfen. Die Böden in 1 l kaltes Wasser mit der Ascorbinsäure legen, sodass sie leicht bedeckt sind. Gemüse putzen und fein würfeln. Schalotten und Knoblauch schälen und ebenfalls fein würfeln.

Die Artischockenböden abtropfen lassen, klein schneiden und zusammen mit der Pancetta in 3 EL Olivenöl anbraten. Gemüse und Knoblauch zugeben, mit Hühnerbrühe, Weißwein sowie Wermut aufgießen und alles zur Hälfte einkochen. Koriander, Zitronensaft und Lorbeerblatt zugeben.

Mit Pfeffer würzen und weitere ca. 20 Min. leicht köcheln lassen. Anschließend mit dem restlichen Olivenöl verfeinern und die Oliven zugeben. Die Rotbarben waschen, trocken tupfen, innen und außen mit Salz und Pfeffer würzen und mit Zitronensaft beträufeln. Den Knoblauch schälen. Die Fische in einer Pfanne in Olivenöl anbraten, Knoblauchzehen und Kräuterzweige zugeben. Die Fische während des Bratvorgangs mit einem Topf beschweren und von beiden Seiten ca. 3 – 4 Min. braten.

Zum Servieren das Gemüse auf einer Platte anrichten, den Fisch darauf geben und diesen mit der Pancetta belegen.

Tipp: Dazu passen selbstgemachte Thymiangnocchi.

The award-winning restaurant of the Käfer delicatessen company consists of a main restaurant and twelve separate rooms. The main restaurant has an open kitchen and a minimalist decor. Fine materials harmonize with bucolic elements in its contemporary Bavarian-oriented design. Each of its separate rooms has its own theme, such as "Wedding," "Bavaria" or "Hunting." It offers high-end international cuisine exhibiting utmost product quality based on the seasons as well as a fine assortment of wines.

Das hochdekorierte Restaurant des Feinkosthauses Käfer besteht aus einem Hauptrestaurant und zwölf Stuben. Das Hauptrestaurant hat eine offene Küche, sein Dekor ist minimalistisch. Im zeitgenössisch bayerisch orientierten Design harmonieren edle Materialien mit rustikalen. Die Stuben sind thematisch gestaltet, nach Themen wie „Hochzeit", „Bayern" oder „Jagd". Geboten wird gehobene internationale Küche, die von höchster Produktqualität zeugt und saisonal orientiert ist. Das Weinangebot ist gut sortiert.

Bastian Falkenroth
K&K KOCHBAR
Hamburg, Germany

It takes nerves of steel to allow customers to watch your every move while you're doing your job. Bastian Falkenroth doesn't mind letting people peer into his cooking pots: he has been managing the open show kitchen of the *K&K KOCHBAR* since the beginning of 2007. Here the guests can gain fascinating insights into the way the Head Chef and his team work. Born in Aachen he learnt to cook from scratch at *Le Moissonnier* in Cologne, *La Table* in Dortmund as well as *La Vie* in Osnabrück, among others. His original creations are characterized by a successful combination of tradition and innovation. The young Head Chef pulls out all the stops using the most interesting international cooking trends to create tempting new dishes. Their cutting-edge presentation add a certain "je ne sais quoi" to the dining experience. In a nutshell: Bastian Falkenroth's authentic combination of a feast for both the eyes and palate is very convincing.

Es braucht schon eine gewisse Portion Nervenstärke, wenn einem täglich die Kunden bei der Arbeit auf die Finger schauen. Bastian Falkenroth lässt sich gerne in die Töpfe gucken: Seit Anfang 2007 leitet er die offene Show-Küche der *K&K KOCHBAR*, wo die Gäste einen spannenden Einblick in die Arbeitsweise des Küchenchefs und seiner Mitarbeiter bekommen. Der gebürtige Aachener hat das Kochen von der Pike auf gelernt, unter anderem im *Le Moissonnier* in Köln, im *La Table* in Dortmund sowie im *La Vie* in Osnabrück. Seine einfallsreichen Kreationen zeichnen sich durch die gelungene Kombination von Tradition und Moderne aus. Der junge Küchenchef zieht dabei alle Register der weltweit interessantesten Kochtrends und schafft verführerische neue Gerichte. Ihre innovative Präsentation macht dabei einen zusätzlichen Reiz aus. Kurz gesagt: Bastian Falkenroth überzeugt durch die authentische Synthese von kulinarischem Hochgenuss und Augenschmaus.

Tataki of Wagyu Beef Seasoned with Charcoal Oil

Serves 8

Charcoal oil
½ c 2 tbs Alba oil (rapeseed oil)
1 ½ oz charcoal

Potato chips
2 oz La Ratte potatoes
vegetable fat for frying

Wagyu beef
13.3 oz Wagyu sirloin
maldon sea salt
sansho pepper
1 box of cress

Heat the rapeseed oil to 140 °F. Break the charcoal into small pieces and pour the heated oil over it. Leave covered to soak for approx. 24 hours and then strain.

Wash the potatoes and cut them unpeeled into thin slices or shreds. Leave to soak in cold water for approx. 30 min. Dab dry and then fry in the hot vegetable fat until golden brown.

Trim the rack of Wagyu beef and then cut into 8 equally-sized pieces using a sharp knife (approx. 2 oz each). Sauté on both sides in a non-stick coated pan. Quench in ice-cold water and dab dry.

Cut each piece of meat into 8 wafer-thin slices and serve on a plate. Sprinkle with 2 tsp of charcoal oil and season with Maldon sea salt and Sansho pepper. Decorate with the potato chips and cress.

Info: Tataki refers to a Japanese form of preparation similar to Carpaccio.

Tataki vom Wagyu-Beef mit Holzkohleöl

Für 8 Portionen

Holzkohleöl
150 ml Albaöl
50 g Holzkohle

Kartoffelchips
60 g La Ratte-Kartoffeln
Pflanzenfett zum Frittieren

Wagyu-Beef
400 g Wagyu-Rücken
Maldon Sea Salt
Japanischer Bergpfeffer
1 Kästchen Kresse

Das Albaöl auf 60 °C erwärmen, die Holzkohle in kleinere Stücke zerteilen und mit dem erwärmten Öl übergießen. Zugedeckt ca. 24 Std. ziehen lassen und anschließend passieren.

Die Kartoffeln waschen und mit der Schale in dünne Scheiben schneiden oder hobeln. In kaltem Wasser etwa 30 Min. ziehen lassen. Anschließend gut trocken tupfen und im heißen Fett goldgelb frittieren.

Den Wagyu-Rücken parieren und mit einem scharfen Messer in 8 gleichgroße Stücke (à ca. 50 g) schneiden. In einer heißen beschichteten Pfanne von allen Seiten kurz anbraten. Anschließend in Eiswasser abschrecken und trocken tupfen.

Das Fleisch in je 8 hauchdünne Scheiben schneiden und auf einem Teller anrichten. Mit jeweils 2 EL Holzkohleöl beträufeln und mit Maldon Sea Salt und Bergpfeffer würzen. Mit den Kartoffelchips und Kresseblättchen dekorieren.

Info: Tataki bezeichnet eine japanische Zubereitungsart ähnlich dem Carpaccio.

The **K&K KOCHBAR** combines art and fine cuisine in a casual fine dining setting. The dining room with its gallery-style interior masterfully displays works of art by renowned artists and comfortably seats up to 70 people. The open kitchen allows the guests to be at the heart of the action and watch the chefs preparing the meals. All dishes are available in two different portion sizes and the wine list offers a selection of over 60 excellent wines by the glass. You can book the *K&K KOCHBAR* exclusively for your private function for up to 150 guests at the *Curiohaus*, a venue which also hosts events for up to 1000 people.

Kunst und feine Küche vereinen sich in der *K&K KOCHBAR* bei „Casual Fine Dining". 70 Sitzplätze bietet der im Stil einer Galerie ausgestatte Raum, in dem Werke namhafter Künstler gekonnt in Szene gesetzt werden. Man steht im unmittelbaren Kontakt mit den Köchen, die in der offenen Showküche bei der Arbeit beobachtet werden können. Speisen können in zwei verschiedenen Portionsgrößen gewählt werden, die Karte bietet eine Auswahl von über 60 erlesenen Weinen im offenen Ausschank. Auch exklusiv für Veranstaltungen bis zu 150 Personen ist die *K&K KOCHBAR* im *Curiohaus* buchbar, welches parallel Veranstaltungsmöglichkeiten für bis zu 1000 Personen bietet.

Jan Kvasnička
Lary Fary
Prague, Czech Republic

Jan Kvasnička is Head Chef at *Lary Fary* where diners are given the chance to travel around the world every time they visit. Born in the town of Chrudim and graduate of the Culinary Academy, Kvasnička's cooking experience began with French cuisine at the *Municipal House* in Prague. He went on to work in Italy, then Australia at Restaurant *Iceberg* in Sydney under Robert Marchetti, holder of "2 Chef's Hats" for his Mediterranean menu as judged by the Sydney Morning Herald. He later returned to French cuisine, joining Sydney's equally rated Restaurant *Forty One* under Dietmar Sawyere. At *Lary Fary*, Kvasnička is regarded as a truly "modern gourmet," excelling through the creation of a diverse spectrum of dishes from the preparation of seafood and exotic freshwater fish to traditional Czech cuisine.

Jan Kvasnička ist Chefkoch bei *Lary Fary*, einem Restaurant, das seinen Gästen bei jedem Besuch die Möglichkeit bietet, kulinarisch um die Welt zu reisen. In Chrudim geboren, absolvierte Kvasnička die Culinary Academy und sammelte seine ersten Kocherfahrungen in der französischen Küche im *Municipal House* in Prag. Anschließend arbeitete er zunächst in Italien, später im Restaurant *Iceberg* in Sydney, unter der Anleitung von Robert Marchetti, der für seine mediterrane Küche vom Sydney Morning Herald mit „2 Kochmützen" ausgezeichnet wurde. Sein weiterer Weg führte ihn zu Dietmar Sawyere ins ebenfalls ausgezeichnete Restaurant *Forty One*, womit Kvasnička sich wieder der französischen Küche zuwandte. Im *Lary Fary* gilt Kvasnička als ein wahrer, „moderner Gourmet", der sich durch seine Bandbreite an unterschiedlichen Gerichten auszeichnet – von Meeresfrüchten über exotische Süßwasserfische bis hin zur traditionellen tschechischen Küche.

Roasted Filet of Pork with Shallot Confit Served with Grilled Polenta and Mushroom Sauce

Serves 2

¾ c vegetable stock
1 ½ oz polenta
4 shallots
6 ½ oz pork filet
salt, pepper
4 tbs olive oil
sugar
3 ½ tbs white wine
6 ½ oz mixed button mushrooms
1 ½ oz butter
½ c beef stock

Boil the vegetable stock, stir in the polenta and leave to soak for 5 min. Then spread thinly into a square on a plastic wrap, leave to cool and chill. Peel the shallots and cut into four.

Season the pork filet with salt and pepper and sear on both sides in a pan with olive oil. Then remove from the pan and place into an ovenproof dish. Sauté the shallots in a pan and season with salt, pepper and a pinch of sugar. Deglaze with white wine, add to the pork filets and roast in a convection oven for 40 min. at 160 °F.

Clean the mushrooms and cut into small pieces. Sauté in butter and add the beef stock. Bring to a boil and reduce liquid to a third. Season to taste with salt and pepper and thicken the sauce with the remaining butter.

Cut the polenta into four squares and sauté in olive oil until golden brown. Cut the pork filet into four pieces and season with salt and pepper.

Place 1 slice of polenta in the middle of each plate, put the shallots on top and cover with another slice of polenta. Serve two pieces of the meat to the left and right of the polenta respectively. Spread the remaining shallots and mushroom sauce evenly around the polenta and serve immediately.

Gebratenes Schweinefilet mit Schalotten, gebratener Polenta und Pilzsauce

Für 2 Personen

200 ml Gemüsebrühe
50 g Polenta
4 Schalotten
200 g Schweinefilet
Salz, Pfeffer
4 EL Olivenöl
Zucker
50 ml Weißwein
200 g gemischte Champignons
50 g Butter
125 ml Rinderbrühe

Die Gemüsebrühe aufkochen, Polenta einrühren und ca. 5 Min. quellen lassen. Anschließend auf Frischhaltefolie dünn zu einem Rechteck ausstreichen, abkühlen lassen und kalt stellen. Schalotten schälen und vierteln.

Das Schweinefilet mit Salz und Pfeffer würzen und rundherum in 2 EL Olivenöl in einer Pfanne scharf anbraten, herausnehmen und in eine Auflaufform geben. Schalotten in der Pfanne anbraten und mit Salz, Pfeffer und 1 Prise Zucker würzen. Mit Weißwein ablöschen, zum Schweinefilet geben und im Backofen bei 70 °C Heißluft weitere 40 Min. garen.

Die Pilze putzen und klein schneiden. In einer Pfanne in Butter anschwitzen und mit Rinderbrühe aufgießen. Aufkochen und auf ein Drittel der Flüssigkeit reduzieren. Mit Salz und Pfeffer abschmecken und die Sauce mit der restlichen Butter binden.

Die Polenta in 4 Rechtecke schneiden und in Olivenöl von beiden Seiten goldbraun anbraten. Das Schweinefilet in vier Stücke schneiden, salzen und pfeffern.

Je 1 Polentascheibe in der Mitte des Tellers anrichten, Schalottenviertel darauf geben und mit einer weiteren Polentascheibe belegen. Jeweils zwei Fleischstücke links und rechts neben der Polenta anrichten. Restliche Schalotten und Champignonsauce rundherum verteilen und sofort servieren.

The rooms of this restaurant, opened in 2002, are decorated in vivid colors with their own, highly individual designs. The restaurant boasts an eclectic style and each of its rooms utilizes design elements from various cultures such as the Orient or Polynesia. Its cuisine has international and Asian flavors. The *Lary Fary* is especially well known for its barbecue specialties, although its sushi is in high demand too. Its well-arranged wine list also offers domestic wine. Plus, you can enjoy a hookah after your meal.

Die Räume des 2002 eröffneten Restaurants sind in kräftigen Farben und jeweils sehr individuell gestaltet. Der Stil ist eklektisch, und jeder Raum bietet Design-Elemente unterschiedlicher Kulturen, so zum Beispiel orientalische oder polynesische. Die Küche ist international und asiatisch ausgerichtet. Besonders bekannt sind die Grillspezialitäten, aber auch das Sushi ist beliebt. Die gut sortierte Weinkarte bietet auch heimische Weine, und nach dem Essen kann man eine Wasserpfeife genießen.

Masayasu Haruyama
Nishimura
Beijing, China

Masayasu Haruyama is the Chef at *Nishimura* in the *Shangri-La Hotel*, Beijing. He is a newcomer to the Chinese capital and sees the increasing popularity of Japanese food in this thriving metropolis as an opportunity for his creativity and passion for Japanese cuisine to be celebrated. His extensive experience with the exclusive *Hyatt* hotel group in Australia, Guam (USA) and Malaysia has infused him with the flavors of the New World, which he now fully integrates in his creative, though traditional, Asian delicacies. Having spent nine years in Australia, Masayasu has developed a signature style that focuses on taste, flavor and innovative presentation. His ambition is to offer the most authentic Japanese cuisine to his Beijing guests by combining both imported produce and the freshest seasonal local ingredients. At *Nishimura*, Masayasu will showcase his culinary skills at Beijing's first Robatayaki, in addition to the Sushi Bar and Teppanyaki section.

Masayasu Haruyama ist Chefkoch im Restaurant *Nishimura* im *Shangri-La Hotel* in Peking. Er ist erst vor Kurzem in die chinesische Hauptstadt gekommen und ist überzeugt, dass in der boomenden Metropole aufgrund der wachsenden Begeisterung für japanisches Essen seine Kreativität und Leidenschaft für die japanische Küche viele Anhänger finden wird. Bei seiner Arbeit für die Hotelkette *Hyatt* in Australien, Guam (USA) und Malaysia sammelte er wertvolle Erfahrungen und lernte das Geschmacksspektrum der Neuen Welt kennen, das er nun in seine kreativen, dennoch traditionellen asiatischen Spezialitäten einfließen lässt. Masayasu verbrachte neun Jahre in Australien und entwickelte dabei seinen eigenen Stil, der Geschmack, Aroma und innovative Präsentation in den Vordergrund stellt. Sein Ziel ist es, mit einer Kombination aus importierten Produkten und den frischesten lokalen Saisonerzeugnissen seinen Pekinger Gästen eine japanische Küche mit größtmöglicher Authentizität zu bieten. Im *Nishimura* bietet Masayasu, neben der Sushi-Bar und Teppanyaki, nun auch als erster in Peking Robatayaki-Gerichte an.

Broiled Lamb Chop Bacon Roll with Black Sesame Miso

Serves 4

1 ½ oz Dengaku miso
1 ½ oz black sesame paste
2 spring onions
2 ½ oz eggplant
5 tbs oil
3 ½ tbs soy sauce
3 ½ tbs lemon juice
1 tbs honey
½ tsp chili powder
4 lamb chops (approx. 1 ½ oz each)
1 bunch watercress
4 slices bacon

Mix the miso and sesame paste. Clean the spring onions and cut the green parts diagonally into pieces. Cut the eggplant into 8 slices and fry on both sides in a pan with 3 tbs olive oil for approx. 2 min. Remove from the pan and keep warm.

Mix the soy sauce, lemon juice, honey and chili powder and leave the lamb chops to marinate for approx. 3 min. Drain the lamb chops and sauté on both sides in a pan for approx. 2 min. using the remaining oil. Then, wrap in a slice of bacon and fry for a further 4 min.

Spread the sesame miso paste onto four plates. Place 2 slices of eggplant on the paste, then put a lamb chop on top of the eggplant and spread the watercress and pieces of spring onion to decorate. Drizzle with the marinade and serve.

Gegrillte Lammkoteletts in Speckmantel mit schwarzem Sesam-Miso

Für 4 Personen

50 g Dengaku-Miso
50 g schwarze Sesampaste
2 Frühlingszwiebeln
80 g Aubergine
5 EL Öl
50 ml Sojasauce
50 ml Zitronensaft
1 EL Honig
½ TL Chilipulver
4 Lammkoteletts (à ca. 50 g)
1 Bund Brunnenkresse
4 Scheiben Frühstücksspeck

Miso und Sesampaste verrühren. Frühlingszwiebeln putzen und das Grüne schräg in Stücke schneiden. Die Aubergine in 8 Scheiben schneiden, in einer Grillpfanne in 3 EL Öl von beiden Seiten ca. 2 Min. braten, herausnehmen und warm halten.

Für die Marinade Sojasauce, Zitronensaft, Honig und Chilipulver verrühren und die Lammkoteletts für ca. 3 Min. darin einlegen. Die Lammkoteletts etwas abtropfen lassen, von jeder Seite in der Grillpfanne in dem restlichen Öl ca. 2 Min. anbraten. Anschließend in eine Speckscheibe einwickeln. Weitere 4 Min. medium braten.

Die Sesam-Misopaste auf vier Teller streichen. Je 2 Auberginenscheiben auf der Paste anrichten, ein Lammkotelett darauf legen und die Brunnenkresse sowie die Frühlingszwiebelstücke dekorativ darauf verteilen. Etwas Marinade darübergeben und servieren.

Re-opened following an award-winning redesign, *Nishimura* at the *Shangri-La Hotel,* Beijing has confirmed its reputation as one of the best Japanese restaurants in the capital. The interior blends the five elements of wood, stone, glass, water, and metal, inspiring balance between color, aroma, shape and sound. Featuring both kantou (sushi) and kansai (hot) cuisine served at a sleek sake bar, teppan tables and a sushi bar, guests can also sip rare wines from an extensive sake menu or enjoy them blended in one of their signature sake cocktails.

Nach Neugestaltung – die mit einer Auszeichnung belohnt wurde – und Wiedereröffnung wird das zum *Shangri-La Hotel* in Peking gehörende *Nishimura* seinem Ruf als eines der besten japanischen Restaurants der Hauptstadt vollauf gerecht. Das Interieur verbindet die fünf Elemente Holz, Stein, Glas, Wasser und Metall. Farbe, Geruch, Form und Klang harmonieren miteinander. Sowohl Kantou-Gerichte (Sushi) als auch Kansai-Gerichte (scharf) werden an der eleganten Sake-Bar serviert, es gibt Teppan-Tische und eine Sushi-Bar. Die Gäste können sich außerdem exquisite Weine von der umfangreichen Sake-Karte munden lassen oder sie gemischt als einen der typischen Sake-Cocktails genießen.

Francis Mallmann
Patagonia Sur
Buenos Aires, Argentina

Born in Buenos Aires, Francis Mallmann opened his first restaurant in Bariloche, Patagonia aged 18. In the late 70s and 80s he traveled extensively in France training at many of the three star restaurants in Paris, Lyon, and southern France. Back in South America he worked with restaurants on a TV series that was aired for 17 years and filmed all over the world. He has published three books and collaborated on many others, and his name has been branded on cooking equipment and gourmet foods, including Parmalat and Philips. In 1996 he was awarded the Grand Prix de l'Art de la Cuisine in Paris by the International Academy of Gastronomy and he has since been featured widely in the international media, such as The New York Times, Vogue Entertaining, and Food Illustrated. He refers to his cooking style as "classical rebellion" and owns *Patagonia Sur* in La Boca, Buenos Aires; *Garzon* hotel and restaurant, Uruguay; and *1884* restaurant in Mendoza, Argentina.

In Buenos Aires geboren, eröffnete Francis Mallmann bereits im Alter von 18 Jahren sein erstes Restaurant in Bariloche in Patagonien. In den 70er und 80er Jahren unternahm Mallmann ausgedehnte Reisen nach Frankreich und ließ sich in vielen Drei-Sterne-Restaurants in Paris, Lyon und in Südfrankreich schulen. Zurück in Südamerika arbeitete er mit Restaurants an einer Fernsehserie, die 17 Jahre lang ausgestrahlt und für die auf der ganzen Welt gefilmt wurde. Mallmann hat drei Bücher herausgebracht und an vielen weiteren mitgearbeitet, sein Name findet sich auf Kochgeräten von Philips und auf Gourmetessen von Parmalat. 1996 wurde er in Paris von der Académie Internationale de la Gastronomie mit dem Grand Prix de l'Art de la Cuisine ausgezeichnet. Seitdem wird in den internationalen Medien viel über ihn berichtet, z. B. in der New York Times, der Vogue Entertaining und Food Illustrated. Seinen Kochstil bezeichnet er als „klassische Rebellion". Mallmann gehört das *Patagonia Sur* in La Boca in Buenos Aires, das Hotel und Restaurant *Garzon* in Uruguay sowie das Restaurant *1884* in Mendoza, Argentinien.

Humita "Mashed Corn" with Country Bread Toast

Serves 4

8 raw corncobs
2 small onions
1 oz butter
2 c milk
½ bunch basil
salt
1 tsp chili flakes
sugar
4 slices of country bread toast
1 bunch rocket salad

Remove any leaves and fibers from the corncobs and extract the grains of corn. Peel the onions and finely dice them. Melt the butter in a stewpot, add the onions and sweat them. Add the grains of corn and some milk and bring to a boil whilst stirring continuously.

Lower the temperature and cook for approx. 30 min. Stir occasionally and add milk little by little, until the corn is cooked. Wash the basil, shake off the water, pluck the leaves and chop finely.

Puree the corn, season with salt, chili flakes and, if necessary, a little sugar. Mix in the finely chopped basil and serve with toasted wholemeal bread and rocket salad.

Tip: Pre-cooked corncobs will only require half the amount of milk and a cooking time of 10 min.

Humita „Maispüree" mit Vollkorntoast

Für 4 Personen

8 rohe Maiskolben
2 kleine Zwiebeln
30 g Butter
500 ml Milch
½ Bund Basilikum
Salz
1 TL Chiliflocken
Zucker
4 Scheiben Vollkorntoast
1 Bund Rucola

Die Maiskolben von Blättern und Fäden befreien und die Körner herauslösen. Zwiebeln schälen und in feine Würfel schneiden. In einem Schmortopf die Butter zerlassen und die Zwiebelwürfel darin glasig andünsten. Maiskörner und etwas Milch zugeben und unter ständigem Rühren aufkochen.

Bei geringer Hitze ca. 30 Min. kochen. Gelegentlich umrühren und nach und nach die Milch zugeben, bis der Mais gar ist. Basilikum waschen, trocken schütteln, Blätter abzupfen und fein hacken.

Den Mais pürieren, mit Salz, Chiliflocken und eventuell etwas Zucker abschmecken. Fein gehackten Basilikum unterrühren und mit Vollkorntoast sowie Rucola-Salat servieren.

Tipp: Bereits vorgekochte Maiskolben benötigen nur die Hälfte der Milch und eine Garzeit von 10 Min.

Francis Mallmann   113

Located in a historic building, this restaurant was opened by Francis Mallmann, the well-known Chef and restaurant owner. It offers (southern) Argentinean cuisine in a romantic atmosphere. Select regional wines are on the menu. The rooms are furnished in a festive and opulent style, with all kinds of objects and details. For example, the walls of the dining room are covered in leather. A collection of cookbooks with more than 2,000 volumes adorns the room. The bar area is surrounded by a tent.

Das in einem historischen Gebäude angesiedelte Restaurant wurde von Francis Mallmann, dem bekannten Küchenchef und Restaurantbetreiber, eröffnet. Geboten wird (süd-)argentinische Küche in romantischem Ambiente. Ausgewählte regionale Weine stehen auf der Karte. Die Räume sind festlich und opulent eingerichtet, mit allerlei Objekten und Details. So sind die Wände des Speisesaals in Leder gekleidet. Eine Kochbuchsammlung mit mehr als 2.000 Büchern ziert den Raum. Der Barbereich ist von einem Zelt umgeben.

Marco Medaglia
Puro
Jakarta, Indonesia

Marco Medaglia was born in Chieti, Italy and began his culinary journey at the Hotelier School of Pescara aged 14. Cooking has since been his passion, a profession that has taken him to the best restaurants around the world. His trail of experiences ranges from Italy to Germany, Myanmar, and the United States where he introduced gourmet Italian cuisine to one of the finest restaurants in Los Angeles, *Vincenti*. While in the Republic of San Marino he worked at *Nido del Falco* and served famous figures such as football legend Michel Platini and FIFA President Joseph Blatter. It was love at first taste that brought him to Jakarta in 2006 and an encounter with the Ismaya Group and the chef's unique Tiramisu. It landed him the key position at *Puro*, which is famed for its emphasis on pure rustic regional Italian flavors. It is here where Marco influences Jakarta's food enthusiasts with his extraordinary culinary skills and indulges them with his creativity featuring simple yet innovative authentic Italian cuisine, including his Tiramisu.

Marco Medaglia wurde in Chieti, Italien geboren. Sein kulinarischer Werdegang begann im Alter von 14 Jahren auf der Hotelfachschule in Pescara. Seither ist Kochen seine große Leidenschaft und ein Metier, das ihn in die besten Restaurants weltweit brachte. Seine Erfahrungsreise führte ihn von Italien nach Deutschland, nach Myanmar und in die USA, wo er die italienische Gourmetküche in einem der edelsten Restaurants von Los Angeles, dem *Vincenti* einführte. Während seiner Zeit in San Marino kochte er im *Nido del Falco* für so berühmte Persönlichkeiten wie die Fußballlegende Michel Platini und den FIFA-Präsidenten Joseph Blatter. Es war Liebe auf den ersten Biss, die ihn 2006 nach Jakarta führte und zu einem Zusammentreffen mit der Ismaya-Gruppe inklusive dem einzigartigen Tiramisu des Küchenmeisters. Medaglia bekam die Schlüsselstellung im *Puro* übertragen, das berühmt dafür ist, pure und rustikale Aromen der regionalen italienischen Küche in den Mittelpunkt zu stellen. Im *Puro* beeindruckt Medaglia die Feinschmecker von Jakarta mit seinen außergewöhnlichen Kochkünsten und verwöhnt sie mit seinen kulinarischen Schöpfungen, mit einfacher, aber dennoch origineller und authentischer italienischer Küche – sein Tiramisu eingeschlossen.

Beef Cheek and Red Wine Stew

Serves 4

1 lb 2 oz beef cheek meat
2 onions
3.3 oz carrots
3.3 oz celery
2 garlic cloves
flour for dusting
3 tbs olive oil
2 tbs tomato paste
2 rosemary sprigs
1 bay leaf
salt and pepper
1 ¼ c red wine
2 c beef stock

Cut beef cheeks into 1½-in. cubes. Wash, peel and dice vegetables. Peel garlic and dice finely. Dust beef in flour, place in a pot and fry in 2 tbs of olive oil, then set aside.

Heat the remaining olive oil and cook the garlic and vegetables. Add the tomato paste, herbs and meat, then season with salt and pepper. Add a splash of wine and cover with beef stock. Bring to a boil and simmer gently for 2 hours until the meat is nice and tender. Season to taste before serving.

Tip: Serve with truffle infused potato puree.

Kalbsbackeneintopf in Rotweinsauce

Für 4 Personen

500 g Kalbsbacken
2 Zwiebeln
100 g Karotten
100 g Staudensellerie
2 Knoblauchzehen
Mehl zum Wenden
3 EL Olivenöl
2 EL Tomatenmark
2 Zweige Rosmarin
1 Lorbeerblatt
Salz, Pfeffer
300 ml Rotwein
500 ml Kalbsfond

Die Kalbsbacken in ca. 4 cm große Würfel schneiden. Gemüse putzen, schälen und klein würfeln. Den Knoblauch schälen und ebenfalls in feine Würfel schneiden. Das Fleisch in Mehl wenden und in einem Topf in 2 EL Olivenöl kräftig anbraten. Anschließend herausnehmen.

Das restliche Olivenöl erhitzen, Knoblauch und Gemüse darin anbraten. Tomatenmark und Kräuter zusammen mit dem Fleisch zugeben und mit Salz und Pfeffer würzen. Mit Rotwein ablöschen und Kalbsfond zugießen. Anschließend aufkochen und bei geringer Hitze ca. 2 Std. kochen lassen, bis das Fleisch schön zart ist. Vor dem Servieren nochmals abschmecken.

Tipp: Servieren Sie dazu mit Trüffelpaste verfeinertes Kartoffelpüree.

The **Puro**—**the sibling** restaurant to the *Dragonfly* and *Blowfish*—serves regional Italian specialties that are authentic, old-fashioned, simple and delicious. Its selection of wines is respectable. As its name implies, the restaurant leans towards purist design, with a clear, tasteful-elegant decor. Its interior is kept in white. Baroque and modern elements complement each other in a harmonious whole. The restaurant offers 70 seats with live piano music. DJs spin music tracks in the bar area.

Im *Puro* – dem Schwesterlokal von *Dragonfly* und *Blowfish* – werden regionale italienische Spezialitäten serviert, die unverfälscht, rustikal, simpel und gut sind. Die Weinauswahl ist hervorragend. Wie schon der Name verrät, gibt sich das Lokal eher puristisch, mit klarem, dezent-elegantem Design. Das Interieur ist in Weiß gehalten. Barocke und moderne Elemente ergänzen sich zu einem harmonischen Ganzen. Das Restaurant bietet 70 Plätze, gespielt wird Live-Piano-Musik. Im Barbereich legen DJs auf.

Pierre Gagnaire
Sketch

London, UK

Pierre Gagnaire is Consultant Chef at *Sketch* where his witty, elegant and creative dishes convey a profound understanding of ingredients and how they work together. Admired by his peers and celebrated in the international food press, he has deservedly earned huge respect for his professionalism and innovative cuisine. Born in Apinac, France, Gagnaire has been immersed in restaurants all his life, including his father's restaurant *Le Clos Fleury* near St Etienne, where he retained its Michelin star status. In 1980 he set up his first restaurant in St Etienne, gaining a second Michelin star in 1986 and a third star in 1993. He then moved to Paris and regained his three-star status by 1998 for his restaurant in *Hotel Balzac*. In December 2002 he launched *Sketch* in London with Mourad Mazouz. He has since opened prominent restaurants in Tokyo, Hong Kong, and the predominantly fish restaurant *Gaya* in Paris, which subsequently earned a Michelin star.

Pierre Gagnaire hat die Position des Consultant Chefs im *Sketch* inne. Seine geistreichen, eleganten und kreativen Gerichte zeugen von einer ausgeprägten Kenntnis der Zutaten und deren Zusammenspiel. Von seinen Kollegen bewundert, von der internationalen Gastronomie-Presse gefeiert, hat er für seine Professionalität und seine innovative Küche zu Recht hohes Ansehen erworben. Gagnaire wurde in der französischen Stadt Apinac geboren und ist sein ganzes bisheriges Leben Restaurants verbunden. Darunter auch dem Restaurant seines Vaters, dem *Le Clos Fleury* in der Nähe von Saint-Etienne, dessen Michelin-Stern er mit Erfolg verteidigte. 1980 eröffnete Gagnaire sein erstes eigenes Restaurant in Saint-Etienne und wurde 1986 mit einem zweiten, 1993 mit einem dritten Michelin-Stern belohnt. Es folgte der Umzug nach Paris, wo er 1998 mit seinem Restaurant im *Hotel Balzac* erneut Drei-Sterne-Status erlangte. Im Dezember 2002 eröffnete er zusammen mit Mourad Mazouz das *Sketch* in London. Seither hat Gagnaire herausragende Restaurants in Tokio, Hongkong und das überwiegend auf Fisch spezialisierte Restaurant *Gaya* in Paris eröffnet. Letzteres darf sich mit einem Michelin-Stern schmücken.

Lecture Room Club Sandwich

Serves 4

1 romaine lettuce
3.3 oz scallions
2 tsp pitted black olives
7 ½ oz dried tomatoes
¾ oz garlic cloves
¾ oz Thai basil
10 oz toast
½ c 2 tbs tomato juice
⅓ c 2 tbs milk
⅓ c 2 tbs olive oil
6 ½ oz paper-thin slices of Jabugo ham
1 corn poulard breast (6 ½ oz each)
olive oil to fry
Espelette pepper
juice of 1 lime
juice of 1 lemon
10 oz raw giant prawns (peeled)
3.3 oz mayonnaise
2 tsp Dijon mustard
¾ oz cream
¾ oz raw spaghetti
vegetable oil to poach
1 ½ tbs balsamic vinegar
2 tsp Maldon Sea Salt
1 tsp black pepper
2 tsp chervil
¾ oz edible flowers

Clean, wash and spin-dry the romaine lettuce, then set aside. Finely dice the scallions, olives, dried tomatoes and peeled garlic cloves. Wash and shake-dry the Thai basil. Pluck the basil leaves from its stem and chop them finely. Cut the toast into cubes. Marinate ⅓ of the toast cubes with tomato juice, another ⅓ with milk and garlic, and the rest with olive oil and half of the Thai basil for about 1 hour. Afterwards, transfer the toast cubes to a baking tray covered with parchment paper and dry them in a preheated convection oven at 212 °F for about 20 min. Then remove and let cool.

In a pan, fry the ham without grease until crisp, then let drain on paper towels and roughly break into pieces. Poach the corn poulard breast in olive oil with Espelette pepper, lemon juice and lime juice at 140 °F until cooked through. Then let cool and cut into thin slices. Fry the giant prawns in olive oil. Then transfer them to a bowl and add oil, the remaining Thai basil and Espelette pepper to marinate. Mix mayonnaise with Dijon mustard and cream. Deep-fry the spaghetti until golden and let drain on paper towels.

In a bowl, add all ingredients except the romaine lettuce, spaghetti, chervil and edible flowers and mix well. To arrange the plates, place some of the mixture with 1 romaine lettuce leaf on each plate. Repeat this operation three times. Arrange the other plates equally. Then garnish each plate with 3 spaghetti, 1 chervil leaf and 1 edible flower and serve.

Lecture Room Club Sandwich

Für 4 Personen

1 Romana-Salat
100 g Frühlingszwiebeln
10 g entsteinte, schwarze Oliven
230 g getrocknete Tomaten
20 g Knoblauchzehe
20 g Thai-Basilikum
300 g Toastbrot
150 ml Tomatensaft
100 ml Milch
100 ml Olivenöl
200 g hauchdünne Scheiben Jabugo-Schinken
1 Maispoulardenbrust (à 200 g)
Olivenöl zum Braten
Piment d'espelette
Saft von 1 Limone
Saft von 1 Zitrone
300 g geschälte, rohe Riesengarnelen
100 g Mayonnaise
10 g Dijon-Senf
20 g Sahne
20 g rohe Spaghetti
Pflanzenöl zum Pochieren
20 ml Balsamico-Essig
10 g Maldon Sea Salt
5 g schwarzer Pfeffer
10 g Kerbel
20 g essbare Blüten

Den Romana-Salat putzen und waschen, trocken schleudern und beiseite stellen. Frühlingszwiebel, Oliven, getrocknete Tomaten und geschälten Knoblauch fein würfeln. Thai-Basilikum waschen, trocken schütteln, Blätter abzupfen und hacken. Das Brot in Würfel schneiden. Ein Drittel davon in dem Tomatensaft einlegen, ein weiteres in Milch und Knoblauch, das letzte Drittel in Olivenöl mit der Hälfte Thai-Basilikum. Alles ca. 1 Std. marinieren. Anschließend die Brotwürfel auf einem mit Backpapier ausgelegten Backblech im vorgeheizten Backofen bei 100 °C Heißluft ca. 20 Min. trocknen. Herausnehmen und abkühlen lassen.

Den Schinken in einer Pfanne ohne Fett knusprig ausbraten, auf Küchenpapier abtropfen lassen und grob zerteilen. Die Maispoulardenbrust in Olivenöl mit Piment d'espelette, Zitronen- und Limonensaft bei 60 °C pochieren, bis sie gar ist. Anschließend abkühlen lassen und in dünne Scheiben schneiden. Die Riesengarnelen in Olivenöl braten. Dann mit dem Öl, restlichem Basilikum und Piment d'espelette in eine Schüssel geben und darin marinieren. Die Mayonnaise mit Dijon-Senf und Sahne verrühren. Spaghetti goldgelb frittieren und auf Küchenpapier abtropfen lassen.

Alle Zutaten – ohne Romana-Salat, Spaghetti, Kerbel und Blüten – in eine Schüssel geben und gut mischen. Zum Anrichten etwas von der Mischung auf einen Teller geben, mit 1 Romana-Salatblatt belegen und diesen Vorgang noch drei Mal wiederholen. Die restlichen Teller genauso anrichten. Anschließend mit jeweils 3 Spaghetti, 1 Kerbelblatt und 1 essbaren Blüte garnieren und servieren.

Award-winning chef Pierre Gagnaire and his design team have transformed a historic town house into a first-rate temple of gastronomy—with restaurants, bars, a tearoom and a gallery. All offer a la carte dining, while the Lecture Room & Library also serves a set lunch. The innovative French cuisine is excellent and the design of the establishment between art and kitsch is worth a visit: from its Louis XIV interior to its LED installations, plastic coffee spots on its stairs to its bathroom stalls shaped like giant eggs. The Lecture Room & Library at *Sketch* was awarded its first Michelin star in 2005.

Sternekoch Pierre Gagnaire und sein Design-Team haben ein historisches Stadthaus in einen erstklassigen Gastrotempel verwandelt – mit Restaurants, Bars, Tea Room und Galerie. Man kann überall à la carte essen, während Lecture Room & Library auch ein festes Mittagsmenü anbietet. Die innovative französische Küche ist exzellent, und das Design des Lokals zwischen Kunst und Kitsch sehenswert: von Louis-XIV-Interieur über LED-Installationen, Plastik-Kaffeeflecken auf der Treppe bis hin zu Toilettenkabinen in Form riesiger Eier. The Lecture Room & Library im *Sketch* wurden 2005 mit dem ersten Michelin-Stern ausgezeichnet.

Jean-Georges Vongerichten
Spice Market
New York, USA

Jean-Georges Vongerichten was born near Strasbourg in Alsace, France. He trained at the *Auberge de l'Ill* and as an apprentice to Chef Paul Haeberlin, then with Paul Bocuse, and later with Master Chef Louis Outhier at *L'Oasis* in southern France. His three-star Michelin training led him to Asia and positions in the *Oriental Hotel* in Bangkok, the *Le Méridien Hotel* in Singapore and the *Mandarin Oriental Hotel* in Hong Kong. Having developed a love for the aromatic flavors of the East, his signature "vibrant cuisine" features intense flavors and satisfying textures from vegetables, juices, and fruit essences, light broths and herbal vinaigrettes. With a string of renowned restaurants in the USA, Europe, and China, he earned six Michelin stars in 2007. Besides numerous TV appearances, he is Chef in Residence for City magazine, and Master Cook for Food & Wine magazine. He has also authored several cookbooks including the recently published "Asian Flavors of Jean-Georges," featuring recipes from his restaurants *Spice Market* and *Vong*.

Jean-Georges Vongerichten wurde im Elsass, in der Nähe von Straßburg geboren. Er lernte in der *Auberge de l'Ill* und war Auszubildender bei Paul Haeberlin, später unter Paul Bocuse und schließlich im *L'Oasis* in Südfrankreich bei Meisterkoch Louis Outhier. Seine Ausbildung führte ihn nach Asien und brachte ihm Anstellungen im *Oriental Hotel* in Bangkok, im *Le Méridien Hotel* in Singapur und im *Mandarin Oriental Hotel* in Hongkong ein. Vongerichten entwickelte eine Vorliebe für die würzigen Aromen des Ostens; seine charakteristische „pulsierende Küche" setzt auf den intensiven Geschmack und ein zufriedenstellendes Zusammenspiel von Gemüse, Säften, Fruchtessenzen und Kräutervinaigretten. Mit einer Reihe renommierter Restaurants in den USA, Europa und China hat Vongerichten 2007 sechs Michelin-Sterne beanspruchen können. Neben zahlreichen Fernsehauftritten ist er auch Chef in Residence für das Magazin City und Master Cook für die Zeitschrift Food & Wine. Des Weiteren hat er diverse Kochbücher verfasst, u. a. das kürzlich veröffentlichte „Asian Flavors of Jean-Georges", das Rezepte aus seinen Restaurants *Spice Market* und *Vong* vorstellt.

Rice Cracker Crusted Tuna with Sriracha-Citrus Emulsion

Serves 4

1 tbs bonito flakes
4 egg yolks
⅓ c 2 tbs freshly squeezed lime juice
3 ½ tbs freshly squeezed orange juice
¼ c Sriracha sauce
3 ½ tsp salt
¼ c pumpkin seed oil
4 tuna filets (2 ½ oz each)
3 oz egg whites
5 tbs cornstarch
5 ½ oz rice crackers
oil to deep-fry
2 scallions

Heat ⅗ cup of water to 185 °F, add the bonito flakes, and let stand for 10 min. Then strain the flakes through a sieve and retain the liquid. Crush the flakes. Measure ¼ cup of the liquid and puree it with egg yolks, lime juice, orange juice, Sriracha sauce and salt in a food processor. Pour in the oil a little at a time, and then set aside to cool.

Cut the tuna filets into slices of 2 ⅓ in. length, ½ in. width and ½ in. thickness. Beat the egg white with cornstarch until the mixture is smooth. Crush the rice crackers into crumbs. Dip tuna in the egg-starch mixture, then roll it in the cracker crumbs. Deep-fry the tuna for approx. 25 seconds until golden brown on the outside, but raw on the inside. Clean, wash and chop the scallions into small pieces, then add them to the sriracha-citrus emulsion.

Arrange the emulsion on plates along with the tuna and serve.

Thunfisch mit Reiskräcker-Kruste und Sriracha-Zitrusfrucht-Emulsion

Für 4 Personen

14 g Bonito-Flocken
4 Eigelb
100 ml frisch gepresster Limettensaft
50 ml frisch gepresster Orangensaft
60 ml Sriracha
18 g Salz
60 ml Kürbiskernöl
4 Thunfischfilets (à 80 g)
85 g Eiweiß
65 g Maisstärke
150 g Reiskräcker
Öl zum Frittieren
2 Frühlingszwiebeln

150 ml Wasser auf ca. 85 °C erhitzen und über die Bonito-Flocken geben. 10 Min. ziehen lassen, in ein Sieb geben und den Fond dabei auffangen. Die Flocken ausdrücken, 60 ml von dem Fond abmessen und mit Eigelb, Limetten- und Orangensaft, Sriracha und Salz in einer Küchenmaschine pürieren. Nach und nach das Öl einfließen lassen, anschließend kalt stellen.

Thunfisch in 6 cm lange, 1,5 cm breite und 1,5 cm hohe Stücke schneiden. Das Eiweiß mit der Maisstärke zu einer geschmeidigen Masse aufschlagen. Die Reiskräcker zerbröseln. Den Thunfisch durch die Ei-Stärke-Masse ziehen und in den Bröseln wenden. Für ca. 25 Sek. frittieren, so dass der Thunfisch außen goldbraun, aber innen noch roh ist. Die Frühlingszwiebeln putzen, waschen, in Röllchen schneiden und in die Emulsion geben.

Zusammen mit dem Thunfisch auf Tellern anrichten und servieren.

You can immediately sense a passion for East-Asian flair and bazaars in this hot spot in the Meatpacking District. The seats in the restaurant are arranged into smaller niches around an atrium, offering a view of the bar. It boasts original Oriental decor, subtle lighting and rooms with soft colors. Jean-Georges Vongerichten and his team will pamper you with sophisticated, exotic dishes and sweep you away into a world of spice combinations you never would have dreamed of.

In diesem Hotspot im Meatpacking District ist die Leidenschaft für ostasiatisches Flair und für Basare sofort spürbar. Die Sitzplätze im Restaurant sind in kleineren Nischen und um ein Atrium angeordnet, mit Blick auf die Bar. Die Einrichtung ist original orientalisch, die Beleuchtung dezent, und die Räume sind in sanften Farben gehalten. Jean-Georges Vongerichten und sein Team verwöhnen hier mit raffinierten, exotischen Gerichten und entführen ihre Gäste in eine Welt ungeahnter Gewürzkombinationen.

Khor Eng Yew
Zheng He's
Dubai, United Arab Emirates

Khor Eng Yew has risen through the ranks of the restaurant profession by working in the kitchens of some of Asia's premium hotel groups such as the *Mandarin Oriental* and *Shangri-La*. Before joining *Zheng He's* in 2007, he was employed at *Shangri-La's Mactan Island Resort & Spa* where he oversaw the opening of the *Tea of Spring* Chinese restaurant and contributed to the success of several prominent events including the 12th ASEAN Summit. As Executive Chinese Chef at *Zheng He's* in the *Madinat Jumeirah Resort*, he has quickly established a reputation for delivering exquisite Chinese a-la-carte cuisine.

Khor Eng Yew hat sich durch seine Tätigkeit in den Küchen einiger erstklassiger Hotelgruppen Asiens, wie *Mandarin Oriental* und *Shangri-La*, nach ganz oben gearbeitet. Bevor er 2007 zum *Zheng He's* kam, war seine Wirkungsstätte das *Shangri-La's Mactan Island Resort & Spa*, wo er für die Eröffnung des chinesischen Restaurants *Tea of Spring* verantwortlich war und zum Erfolg diverser bedeutender Veranstaltungen, wie dem 12. ASEAN-Gipfel, beitrug. Als Executive Chinese Chef im *Zheng He's* im *Madinat Jumeirah Resort* hat er sich, dank seiner exquisiten chinesischen À-la-carte-Küche, schnell einen hervorragenden Ruf erworben.

Beef Filet with Black Pepper Sauce

Serves 4

Sauce
1 ½ oz shallots
1 ½ oz garlic cloves
1 ½ oz butter
2 ½ oz black peppercorns
2 ½ oz tomato ketchup
1 c water
3 tbs Worcester sauce
⅓ c 2 tbs Maggi seasoning
3.3 oz sugar beet syrup
⅓ c 2 tbs oyster sauce
½ c instant chicken bouillon
1 tbs flour
1 tbs corn oil

Beef Filet
1 ½ oz garlic cloves
3.3 oz red onions
3.3 oz shallots
2 scallions
3.3 oz yellow bell peppers
1 lb 2 oz filet of beef
2 tbs corn oil
salt, pepper
¾ c black pepper sauce
½ tbs rice wine (Hua Tiao)
pink pepper berries

For the sauce: peel and finely chop the shallots and garlic cloves. Heat a little butter in a wok and gently sauté the shallots and garlic in it. Add the remaining ingredients except flour and corn oil and bring to a boil. Combine flour and corn oil to a good mixture and add it little by little with continuous stirring to the boiling liquid until the sauce thickens.

For the beef filet: peel the garlic cloves and cut them into slivers. Peel and finely dice the red onions. Also peel and quarter the shallots. Clean the scallions and cut them into small pieces. Clean and roughly dice the bell pepper. Also roughly dice the beef filet. In a wok, heat the oil, sauté garlic, red onions, scallions, yellow bell peppers and shallots and season them with salt and pepper to taste. Then set aside and keep warm.

Cook the beef filet cubes for about 3–4 min. to medium rare and add the pepper sauce. Let boil for about 30 seconds and enhance the flavor with rice wine.

Arrange the vegetables along with the beef filet cubes and pepper sauce on plates, sprinkle with pink pepper berries and serve.

Rinderfilet mit Schwarzpfeffersauce

Für 4 Personen

Soße
50 g Schalotten
50 g Knoblauchzehen
50 g Butter
75 g schwarze Pfefferkörner
75 g Tomatenketchup
250 ml Wasser
40 ml Worcester-Sauce
100 ml Maggi Würze
100 g Zuckerrübensirup
100 ml Austernsauce
40 g Instant-Hühnerbrühe
1 EL Mehl
1 EL Maisöl

Rinderfilet
50 g Knoblauchzehen
100 g rote Zwiebeln
100 g Schalotten
2 Frühlingszwiebeln
100 g gelbe Paprikaschote
500 g Rinderfilet
2 EL Maisöl
Salz, Pfeffer
160 g schwarze Pfeffer-Sauce
½ EL Reiswein (Hua Tiao)
rosa Pfefferbeeren

Für die Sauce Schalotten und Knoblauchzehen schälen und fein hacken. Etwas Butter im Wok erhitzen, Knoblauch und Schalotten darin anbraten. Die restlichen Zutaten, bis auf Mehl und Maisöl, zugeben und aufkochen. Mehl und Maisöl gut vermengen, unter ständigem Rühren nach und nach in die heiße Flüssigkeit geben und kochen lassen, bis die Sauce andickt.

Für das Filet Knoblauchzehen schälen und in feine Scheiben schneiden. Rote Zwiebel und Schalotten ebenfalls schälen. Die Zwiebel fein würfeln, die Schalotten vierteln. Frühlingszwiebeln putzen und in Stücke schneiden. Die Paprikaschote putzen und grob würfeln. Das Rinderfilet ebenfalls grob würfeln. Den Wok erhitzen, Öl zugeben und Knoblauch, rote Zwiebeln, Frühlingszwiebeln, gelbe Paprika und Schalotten kurz braten, mit Salz und Pfeffer abschmecken und warm halten.

Die Rinderfiletwürfel ca. 3 – 4 Min. medium braten und die Pfeffer-Sauce zugeben. Etwa 30 Sek. kochen lassen und mit Reiswein verfeinern.

Das Gemüse auf Tellern mit den Rinderfiletwürfeln und der Pfeffer-Sauce darauf anrichten. Mit rosa Pfefferbeeren bestreut servieren.

Chinese cuisine with Western influences is offered by the restaurant of the *Mina A' Salam* boutique hotel, opened in 2003 as part of the *Madinat Jumeirah Resort*. Glowing red lamps decorate the interior of this restaurant and modern dark furniture contrasts with Oriental rugs. Its premises also boast a bar—as well as a tea counter. *Zheng He's* offers space for about 100 guests and almost 60 more can dine on the spacious terrace with a view of the Arabian Gulf.

Chinesische Küche mit westlichen Einflüssen bietet das Restaurant des 2003 eröffneten Boutiquehotel *Mina A' Salam*, das zum *Madinat Jumeirah Resort* gehört. Leuchtend rote Lampen zieren das Interieur des Lokals, modernes dunkles Mobiliar kontrastiert mit orientalischen Teppichen. In den Räumlichkeiten befinden sich auch eine Bar- sowie eine Teetheke. Gut 100 Gäste haben im Restaurant *Zheng He's* Platz, nahezu 60 weitere können auf der großzügigen Terrasse speisen, mit Blick auf den Arabischen Golf.

Index

The China House, The Oriental Bangkok 38
48 Oriental Avenue, Bangkok 10500, Thailand/Silom
Phone: +66 2 659 9000, www.mandarinoriental.com
Design: Neri and Hu Design and Research Office
Chef: Kong Khai Meng
Owner: The Oriental, Bangkok
Opening hours: Daily, lunch 11.30 am to 2.30 pm, dinner
7 pm to 10.30 pm
Average price: Lunch $ 42, dinner $ 75 (including drinks)
Cuisine: Cantonese
Special features: Freestanding bar, private 'opium bed'
banquettes, Tea Apothecary

FACIL 44
Potsdamer Straße 3 | 10785 Berlin, Germany | Tiergarten
Phone: +49 30 5 90 05 12 34, www.facil.de
Subway: Potsdamer Platz
Design: Ralph Flum
Chef: Michael Kempf
Owner: The Mandala Hotel
Opening hours: Mon–Fri noon to 3 pm, from 7 pm, Sat–Sun closed
Average price: € 30
Cuisine: Mediterranean, classical pure
Special features: Free parking service, glass roof can be opened

Fasano 50
Rua Vittorio Fasano 88 | São Paulo 01414-020, Brazil | Jardins
Phone: +55 11 3062 4000, www.fasano.com.br
Design: Isay Weinfeld
Chef: Salvatore Loi
Owner: Fasano Family
Opening hours: Mon–Sat 7.30 pm to 1 am, Sun closed
Average price: $ 55
Cuisine: Italian
Special features: Bar, hotel

Fifteen 56
15 Westland Place | London N1 7LP, United Kingdom | Islington
Phone: +44 870 787 1515, www.fifteen.net
Subway: Old Street
Design: Bluearc
Chef: Andrew Parkinson
Owner: Fifteen Foundation
Opening hours: Breakfast daily from 7.30 am (8 am on Sun),
lunch daily noon to 3 pm, dinner daily 6.30 pm to 9.45 pm
Average price: Breakfast £ 8, lunch £ 25 to £ 55, dinner £ 25
to £ 70
Cuisine: Modern Mediterranean

Gilt 62
455 Madison Avenue | New York, NY 10022, USA | Midtown
Phone: +1 212 891 8100, www.giltnewyork.com
Subway: 6 51 Street; B, D, F, V 50 Street
Design: Patrick Jouin
Chef: Christopher Lee
Owner: The New York Palace Hotel
Opening hours: Tue–Thu 5:30 pm to 10 pm, Fri–Sat 5.30 pm
to 10.30 pm, Sun + Mon closed; Bar daily from 5 pm to 1 am
Average price: Three Course Prix Fixe Menu $ 78
Cuisine: New American
Special features: Late-night dining

Restaurant Imperial at Hotel Imperial   68
Kärntner Ring 16 | 1015 Vienna, Austria
Phone: +43 15 01 10 356, www.luxurycollection.com/imperial
Chef: Siegfried Kröpfl
Owner: Imperial Hotels Austria AG
Opening hours: Mon–Sun 6 pm to 12 pm
Average Price: Starters 25 €, main course 30 €, 3-course-menu from 59 €
Cuisine: traditional Viennese Cooking with international flair
Special features: 2 toques Gault Millaut

Isola bar & grill   74
Level 3 & 4 ifc Mall, 8 Finance Street | Hong Kong, China | Central
Phone: +852 2383 8765, www.isolabarandgrill.com
Subway: Central
Design: Hugh Zimmern, Leigh & Orange Ltd.
Chef: Giandomenico Caprioli
Owner: Gaia Group
Opening hours: Daily lunch noon to 2:30 pm, dinner Sun–Thu 6:30 pm to 11 pm, Fri–Sat 6:30 pm to 11:30 pm
Average price: Lunch HK$ 250, dinner HK$ 500–600
Cuisine: Italian
Special features: 270° view of harbor, open kitchen

Japonais   80
600 West Chicago Avenue | Chicago, IL 60610, USA
River North Area of Chicago
Phone: +1 312 822 9600, www.japonaischicago.com
Subway: Brown, Purple Line Chicago Station
Design: Jeffrey Beers International
Partners/Chefs: Gene Kato, Jun Ichikawa
Owners: Miae Lim, Rick Wahlstedt, Jeffrey Beers
Opening hours: Lunch Mon–Fri 11:30 am to 2:30 pm, dinner Mon–Thu 5 pm to 11 pm, Fri–Sat 5 pm to 11:30 pm, Sun 5 pm to 10 pm
Average price: $ 27
Cuisine: Contemporary Japanese
Special features: Lounge, fireplace, waterfront terrace

Käfer-Schänke   86
Prinzregentenstraße 73 | 81675 Munich, Germany | Bogenhausen
Phone: +49 89 4 16 82 47, www.feinkost-kaefer.de
Subway: Prinzregentenplatz
Design: Peter Buchberger, Kiki Schröder
Chef: Volker Eisenmann
Owner: Michael Käfer
Opening hours: Mon–Sat 11:30 am to 1 am, closed on Sun
Average price: € 32
Cuisine: International, Mediterranean
Special features: Limousine service

K&K KOCHBAR   92
Curiohaus, Rothenbaumchaussee 11 | 20148 Hamburg, Germany
Phone: +49 40 36 11 16 36, www.koflerkompanie.com
Subway: Dammtorbahnhof
Design: Raumkonzept Balloni ® | Kitchen Gaggenau & Poggenpohl
Chef: Bastian Falkenroth
Owner: KOFLER & KOMPANIE AG
Opening hours: Mon–Sat 6 pm, Sun, noon by appointment only
Average Price: 20 €
Cuisine: Modern, International

Lary Fary 98
Dlouhá 30 | 11 000 Prague, Czech Republic | Prague 1
Phone: +42 022 232 0154, www.laryfary.cz
Subway: Náměstí Republiky
Chef: Jan Kvasnička
Owner: Kolkovna Group a.s.
Opening hours: Daily 11 am to midnight
Average price: 850 Czk
Cuisine: International, Czech, sushi bar

Nishimura, Shangri-La Hotel Beijing 104
29 Zizhuyuan Road | Beijing, 100089 China | Haidian District
Phone: +86 10 6841 2211 extn 6719, www.shangri-la.com
Design: CL3 Architects Ltd
Chef: Masayasu Haruyama
Owner: Shangri-La Hotels and Resorts
Opening hours: Daily, lunch 11.30 am to 2.30 pm, dinner
6 pm to 10 pm
Average price: RMB 500
Cuisine: Japanese
Special features: Traditional Japanese tatami room, over 15 sakes

Patagonia Sur 110
Rocha 803/Pedro de Mendoza | Buenos Aires 1166,

Argentina | La Boca
Phone: +54 11 4303 5917, www.restaurantepatagoniasur.com
Design: Pablo Sanchez Elia, Laura Orcoyen
Chef & Owner: Francis Mallmann
Opening hours: Lunch Tue–Sat noon to 3 pm, dinner 7 pm to
midnight, Sun and Mon closed
Average price: ARS 200
Cuisine: Argentinean
Special features: Exquisite wine list

Puro 116
City Plaza at WISMA MULIA, JI Jend Gatot Subroto Kav 42 |
DKI Jakarta 12710, Indonesia
Phone: +62 21 5297 1234, www.blowfish-puro.com
Design: Sonny Sutanto Architects
Chef: Marco Medaglia
Owner: Ismaya Group
Opening hours: Lunch Mon–Fri 11.30 am to 2.30 pm; dinner
Mon–Sat 6 pm to 11 pm
Average price: $ 35
Cuisine: Italian
Special features: Open kitchen, full bar with live DJ, live piano

Sketch 122
9 Conduit Street | London W1S 2XG, United Kingdom | Mayfair
Phone: +44 207 659 4500, www.sketch.uk.com
Subway: Oxford Circus
Design: Overseen by Mourad Mazouz
Chef & Owner: Pierre Gagnaire
Opening hours: The Gallery Mon–Sat 7 pm to 2 am, The
Lecture Room & Library Tue–Fri noon to 4 pm, Tue–Sat 6:30
pm to midnight, Sun closed
Average price: The Gallery main course £ 25; The Lecture
Room & Library main course £ 48
Cuisine: Modern European
Special features: Art exhibitions

Spice Market   128
403 West 13th Street | New York, NY 10014, USA
Meatpacking District
Phone: +1 212 675 2322, www.jean-georges.com
Subway: A, C, E, L 14 Street
Design: Jacques Garcia
Chef: James Reinholt
Owners: Jean-Georges Vongerichten, Phil Suarez
Opening hours: Sun–Thu noon to midnight, Fri–Sat noon to 1 am
Average price: Lunch $ 37, dinner $ 51
Cuisine: South Eastern Asian
Special features: Late-night dining

Zheng He's   134
Madinat Jumeirah, The Arabian Resort | Mina A'Salam Hotel
PO Box 75157, Dubai, UAE
Phone: +971 4 366 8888
www.madinatjumeirah.com/mina_a_salam/dining/zheng_hes
Design: Khuan Chew of KCA International
Resort Executive Chef: Leslie Stronach
Owner: Jumeirah
Opening hours: Daily lunch noon to 3 pm, dinner 7 pm to
11.30 pm
Average price: AED 300
Cuisine: Modern Chinese
Special features: Terrace